Come to Mary's House

Come to Mary's House

Spending Time with Our Blessed Mother

Shawn Chapman

Our Sunday Visitor
Huntington, Indiana

Nihil Obstat
Msgr. Michael Heintz, Ph.D.
Censor Librorum

Imprimatur
✠ Kevin C. Rhoades
Bishop of Fort Wayne-South Bend
April 29, 2022

The *Nihil Obstat* and *Imprimatur* are
official declarations that a book is free
from doctrinal or moral error. It is not
implied that those who have granted the
Nihil Obstat and *Imprimatur* agree with
the contents, opinions, or statements
expressed.

Our Sunday Visitor Publishing Division
Our Sunday Visitor, Inc.
200 Noll Plaza
Huntington, IN 46750
www.osv.com
1-800-348-2440

ISBN: 978-1-68192-717-6 (Inventory No.
T2589)
1. RELIGION—Christian Living—Spiritual Growth.
2. RELIGION—Christianity—Catholic.
3. RELIGION—Christianity—Saints &
Sainthood.

eISBN: 978-1-68192-718-3
LCCN: 2022939050

Cover design and Interior design: Aman-
da Falk
Cover art: AdobeStock
Interior art: Michelle Mashalei - To order
prints, email michelle.mashalei.art@
gmail.com"

PRINTED IN THE UNITED STATES OF

AMERICA

For my daughters Máire Elizabeth and Róise Mariah

Contents

Introduction

"I've been spending a lot of time in Mary's house," said my friend Nan. "Working in her garden, helping out around the house, having tea in her kitchen. It's been good!" I smiled, imagining the scene: Nan working in the garden with a laughing, muddy, sweaty Virgin Mary, then coming in for a cup of tea. Spending time in Mary's house, as Nan put it, is a lovely metaphor for an intimate, informal friendship with a real, accessible Mary. I was enchanted by the idea. We should all spend time at Mary's house!

We Catholics know Our Lady has a way of bringing us more deeply into the family of her Son. We know she was given to us as our mother when Jesus gave her to John the Apostle from the cross. We know from Revelation that she is the mother of all who follow her Son, and that Scripture says we should honor our mother. We know the early Church gathered around her, relying on her witness and her closeness to Jesus.

But how do we cultivate a relationship with Mary in the course of our normal, day-to-day lives? Is that even possible? I've learned that it's not only possible, it's surprisingly easy — maybe because Mary does most of the work.

Mary can be kind of sneaky, though. I know, because she snuck up on me, and my life has never been the same. I had been raised without religion and was a firm atheist. But when I was nineteen, out of necessity in a time of crisis, I began exploring spirituality. Though I had no intention of having anything to do with any church, I began to be drawn to Mary. Jesus freaked me out. But I was not afraid of Mary.

One day, not knowing why, I walked into Saint Mary's Catholic Church, relieved no one was there so I could look around. I had an experience there I can only describe as being flooded by Mary's love. I knew God was there. As I explained to my mom later, "I could never have made up that kind of love!" Eventually, I realized that if Mary was real, Jesus must be real. I started trying to find ways to relate to him. Pretty soon I found myself at Mass every day, though I still didn't understand why.

I was baptized at a Tuesday evening Mass at Saint Anthony's, hugged enthusiastically by all the old Italian ladies in the front row. Thus definitively began the great romance with the love of my life: Jesus. It turns out Mary tricked me. She will trick you too. You'll love it!

If you long for Mary, if you want to live in spiritual companionship with her, if you want to pray more deeply, love Jesus increasingly, and serve authentically from the heart, you can't find a better master of the spiritual life than Our Lady.

Through the reflections I offer in this book, each followed by a brief imaginative sequence (designed to draw you into prayer, or illustrate some spiritual truth), I hope to open the way for you to a life in her companionship. I hope to help you enjoy a relationship with her, even more than you may already do. She is full of grace, and she wants to share it with you!

Our Lady wants to draw us daily more deeply into union with God. My hope here is to give you the space to meet her … and let her do the rest.

Nan has set the scene for us.

A word about the use of imagination in prayer

Imagine Mary's house in any way that makes sense to you. It

doesn't have to be historically accurate, although sometimes that is helpful. Your ideas of it can change, even from day to day. Maybe you'd like to think of her in her house at Ephesus, where it is thought she went to live with John the Apostle; or at her house in Nazareth; or at a house like the one you grew up in. Really, it can be any architecture of any period of time you'd like.

Try to be receptive, and let an image come to you. That is the most important thing. You don't have to imagine every detail. For me, the best way is to visualize lightly just the few details I need to set me in her presence. I make these as real as I can, and I suggest you do the same. Feel the floor under your feet, note the quality of the light, and any sounds or smells. Notice, perhaps, any spice jars in her kitchen.

This is your beginning. Next, find Mary. What is she doing? Imagine her lightly, too, just enough; her eyes maybe, the way her hair falls, the way her hands feel. You don't need to fill in all the details.

When we imagine lightly like this, we leave room for the Holy Spirit to work. We touch base in our imaginations and then, in a relaxed way, go with it. In the beginning it might help to write down the flow of dialogue or images that come to you, if that helps you stay with the prayer. For me, this is an extremely meaningful and helpful prayer form that can last for a long time.

Sometimes God leads us from this type of prayer into other ways of praying. Let him do that if he wants to. Allow your imagination to fall away, and just be with God or Mary, if that is what starts to happen.

Saint Teresa of Ávila said she didn't exactly imagine a picture of Jesus. For her, it was thinking of him and turning her will and attention toward him in faith that made her prayer and relationship with him grow. Still, she could talk about his "compassionate and lovely eyes." She was not necessarily seeing him in a visual or imaginative way; yet, "dark and lovely" described his eyes for her. She also used images and symbols as a way to describe spiritual realities to the reader. In a way that is what this book will do, too.

One reason imagination is important to what we are doing here is that sometimes the images we may unknowingly have of Mary can be a hindrance in our relationship with her. Shaking up our image of her a little bit can make room for new developments; for her to meet us. Mary's goal is always to draw us more deeply into a relationship with her Son. She has a mysterious way of doing that, and of vivifying our experience of him. Getting to know her in the way she shows you will make your relationship with Jesus more fruitful.

A little imagination can direct our soul's communication in the same way the words of a prayer are a method of directing our attention and will to God. Imagination is an aid to prayer. In time, Mary will fill in the blanks with her own input as we grow in receptivity to her.

M. Mashaei

1
Love Her Like a Sister

Mary can be called daughter of the Church, and our sister as well.

— National Conference of Catholic Bishops
*Behold Your Mother, Woman of Faith: A Pastoral
Letter on the Blessed Virgin Mary*

We are holding hands as we walk together along a rocky path on a hot July evening. We are talking about this and that. She asks me questions and listens thoughtfully as I talk about my life. She has a lot going on too, these days, and she unburdens her heart to me about her work, about her children. I squeeze her hand and we pray together as tears gather in her eyes. I know she works hard for her children and prays constantly for their needs, for their good, for their souls. I am glad she will talk to me about things that concern her, that she finds my company a comfort at times. We lapse into comfortable silence.

She gathers up the brown skirt of her habit a little as we reach an incline, and I smile that she is barefoot like me. Of course she is. People say we resemble one another, especially around the eyes. All of Carmel shares the family resemblance to Mary, our sister, as we share everything else with her. Some might say that ours is a curious Marian devotion, this Carmelite love of Mary not only as mother and queen, but as sister.

Carmelite Marian devotion is primarily about the inner imitation of Mary. We see ourselves as the other Mary, and we view our Carmelite life of prayer and simplicity of heart as a reflection of the interior life she lived and still lives.

More than reflecting on Mary, we desire simply to see through her eyes, love Jesus with her heart, and share in her hidden work in the world — in the silent drawing of her Immaculate Heart of all peoples toward her Son.

Siblings share confidences and understand each other in a special way. They tell each other everything. In intimacy and cooperation with Mary, we receive a double portion of Christ's spirit because she magnifies the Lord. Together with her, we treasure his words and his life continually in our hearts, in union with her.

A sister can share our lives, walk beside us, trust in us, and we in her. Mary doesn't have to knock; she practically lives at our house. When she comes over, she might even fold some of our laundry with us. We are always welcome at Mary's house, too. We are allowed to pick the roses in her garden. She doesn't mind.

Living with her as a sister keeps us in touch with the precious, pure humanity of Mary. It keeps her close by our side, walking with us in a familiar, loving way. We are less likely to only look up to her and more likely to reflect her unconsciously — maybe around the eyes, yes certainly in our ways, surely in the joyful depth of our inner lives in Christ.

As we walk, I notice more and more that there are many others around us. I recognize that it is the craggy path of the ascent of Mount Carmel. We travel with our many brothers and sisters, following Jesus with Mary, our sister, in our midst. She is smiling, enjoying the company, glad we are following her Son all together.

The family of Carmel invites you to love Mary like a sister.

Come to Mary's House

Come in from your walk with Mary. Help her with dinner. Others are helping, too, bringing fruit and wildflowers they have picked, carrying jars of water and jugs of wine. Someone has brought a new baby lamb to introduce to everyone. Together you set the table. Mary is happy, dropping flowers at each one's place. Small clay lamps filled with oil are lit. Everyone sits. The blessing is said. The meal is eaten. One of the friars reads from Holy Scripture. As the reading ends, everyone becomes especially silent, closing their eyes in prayer, and you with them. Now a breeze blows through the house. The little lamps on the table flicker and go out. You can sense that the others are smiling in the dark. God is with you. You smile too.

Read over this again slowly. Stay with this prayer for a moment or two.

2

Look at Mary

"Do you want to see her?" I answered, "Yes, good Lord, thank you very much. Yes, good Lord, if it is your will."

— St. Julian of Norwich
Showings

We can't see Mary physically. However, we can take Saint Teresa of Ávila's advice about friendship with Jesus (*The Way of Perfection*, chapter 25) and apply it also to Our Lady. Saint Teresa suggests we find an image of the Lord that we like, that we are comfortable with. The same advice could apply to Mary. So we would be advised in the beginning to use a painting or statue of her that can be kept near, that we can talk to now and then. Over time such an image migrates into your heart. With a good imagination, you can form a relatable image of Mary in your mind, carrying it with you always, returning to it throughout the day.

One of the ways I approach Mary in friendship is to come to her with a smile. I almost can't think of her without smiling. Can you? When you see your dearest friend, you smile from the heart. If you don't already smile at Mary, doing so can change, slightly, the level of intimacy you feel in her company, which will open your heart a little more to her. She is surely smiling back at you. If your feelings permit, why not smile if you can?

Next, try asking her to journey through this book with you. Tell her what you hope for as you read and pray through it. Be receptive to her as well, and give her time to reciprocate. When speaking with a friend, you would never look around at the trees or at your phone and not at her as you talked to her. In the same way, try to keep your inner vision on Mary when you communicate with her. Keep spiritual "eye contact." Don't worry if this turns out to be harder than you thought. Mary, our friend, is patient and kind. Just return to her as many times as it takes. She'll be there.

While you are saying this silent prayer to Mary and your attention is with her, try also to focus on, and to mean, the words you are saying to her. You wouldn't talk to a friend without even knowing what you were saying. So make an effort to say what you want to say from the heart.

It may surprise you how simple attentiveness brings alive

what is a real encounter. Saint Teresa advises that we humbly ask the Lord for his friendship. So ask Mary too, humbly, for her friendship. The important thing is to "look" at her in the ways that you can. The idea here is to make a connection, to focus your love and attention on her. God will help you. Mary is one of his gifts to us. As Our Lord revealed to St. Julian of Norwich, "After myself, she is the greatest joy I can show you. . . . Of all my creation, she is the most desirable sight" (*Showings*).

Come to Mary's House

She has been waiting for you. She is standing on the threshold of her open door. She holds a hand out to you. Take it in your own, feeling its work-worn roughness and warmth. Greet her with a smile from the heart. Ask for her company. Ask for her friendship. Hear what she says back to you.

M.Mashafei

3
Hail Mary

The glorious Virgin Mary is a most courteous queen, nor, wondrous to say, is it possible to greet her and not be greeted in return. If you say with devotion a thousand "Ave Marias" in a day, a thousand times you will be greeted by the Virgin.

— Saint Bernadino
Opera omnia, 2:154

I remember learning the Hail Mary when I was twenty. I was dating the Catholic boy whom I would one day marry. I was curious about the Hail Mary, never having heard more than the first line of it in movies sometimes, so I asked him to teach it to me. After a few tries, I still wasn't picking it up well. He was frustrated. I asked, "How fast did you pick it up when you learned it?" He said he didn't remember ever not knowing it. I was impressed.

As for me, I received the Hail Mary as something precious

and exotic. Once I finally learned it, I could hardly stop praying it. The words seemed like flowers coming out of my mouth. I went on to learn from him how to pray the Rosary, as I had become fascinated by it. I didn't know what to make of several of the stories to be pondered during its recitation, but I prayed it anyway, making the best of it. I interpreted the mysteries of the Rosary in my own way that made sense to me, until, gently, the stories started to change me. The Gospel became for me, not just an old story I was learning about, but something very present that was happening still, even in my life as I lived it.

At the center of the Hail Mary is Jesus. When I first became interested in the Rosary, I didn't know what to make of him, either. But I held Mary's hand like a child until she led me quietly along in her gentle, inexorable way, to Jesus. In time, through prayer, Word, and Sacrament, and through human love and learning how to pray, I discovered that Jesus is inseparable from life and being itself.

All that Catholic stuff used to seem so repellent to my existentialist and postmodern mindset. But now it's everything to me, because love is what puts us in touch with heaven. I came to love Mary, and all of the rest fell into place.

You can come to Mary in the way that you are able. Just come as you really are. Approach her the way that makes sense to you. That is enough to make a beginning with her. She is gentle and humble of heart, generous with her friendship, and quick to share when she sees an open heart.

Come to Mary's House

You are relieved to be here after a long day at work. The house smells of baking bread. That wonderful aroma nourishes your heart. She is just coming in from the garden with a basket. She greets you as she lays it on the counter. She sees how tired you are. She offers you a chair, makes you a cup of soothing tea. Then she comes to sit with you. Tenderly, she offers you her hands. You take them into your own. She looks at you, perhaps with expectation, maybe with a smile, certainly with love. Holding her hands, keeping your inner gaze on Mary, feeling her warm fingers in yours, say to her a slow, thoughtful Hail Mary. Strive to remain attentive to what you are saying, and to whom you are speaking.

Is there anything else you would like to say to Mary? Does she say anything to you? Rest a moment, now, in her very present love.

4
Mary's Gaze

I am the Immaculate Conception.

— Our Lady to Saint Bernadette

The Church gives us the dogma of Mary's Immaculate Conception to enlighten us on the grace Mary was given from the beginning: freedom from original sin. Pope St. John Paul II said that Adam and Eve originally had "the peace of the interior gaze" (General Audience, January 2, 1980). This means that when Eve and Adam looked at one another, they could each see the inner truth of the other, without experiencing a difference between physical and spiritual sight.

As the "New Eve," free from the sin of our first parents, Mary would have seen people with this interior gaze, too. Undoubtedly this kind of sight is a Gospel way to view other human beings. Jesus, in his teachings, tries to get us to see this way, to live as if we do see this way. Belonging to Jesus leads us to such a vision of others by believing it in faith, hope, and love. Even though we don't literally see on Earth as we will in heaven (though I think falling in love or being a parent sometimes brings us close), we strive to treat others as if we do, letting God begin to draw us ever closer to his own vision.

Mary's freedom from original sin would have given her a gracious core of love, understanding, and acceptance of the people she encountered. Given that gift, how could Mary have failed to love or be merciful toward anyone?

If we all could see within one another and truly understand each other, we wouldn't judge or hate any human being. We would be utterly merciful and forgiving. We would love one another as Christ loves us. We would love our neighbor as ourselves.

As first among the redeemed, and free from original sin in a unique way, Mary would have seen the beauty and Godly purpose in every human being she encountered, as we were all meant to do before the Fall of Adam and Eve. We can be comfortable in Mary's presence because she understands us, she sees us, and she loves us completely and individually.

Come to Mary's House

Sit with Mary. See her looking at you and let yourself be loved and understood by her. Know that her heart is love. She does not judge you, but sees you with the gentle ease of the humble, loving you completely. She sees who you are in God. That is what she sees. Open your heart to her. Stay here as long as you need to, letting her look at you. Holding your gaze on her, pray, "O Mary, conceived without sin, pray for us who have recourse to thee."

5
Mary's Glorified Humanity

Am I not here who am your Mother?

— Our Lady of Guadalupe to St. Juan Diego

Mary is so often portrayed as too pretty to touch, airbrushed like a fluffy cloud or a pink puff of spun cotton candy. But she knew gut-wrenching grief. She cried real tears when she was widowed; of course she did. Joseph's death must have been a bottomless loss for her.

She walked the way of the cross with her Son, wanting to die with him as any mother would. But she stood at the foot of the cross all the same, to love him, and to go on doing whatever he told her. Maybe her toes clenched in her sandals as she stood there; toes that probably looked more like Mother Teresa's than the dainty, artistic feet that peek out from beneath her dress in so many representations. Maybe she took her sandals off, because she knew that Golgotha had just become holy ground.

Mary's humanity is also her glory, to God and to us. It is the way to know her intimately. Her hands, likely bloodied from attempts to comfort her bleeding Son, were probably rough and work-scarred from a lifetime of labor and loving service. These hands of Mary's — the same hands that would be assumed into heaven — had held babies, hauled water, kneaded bread, cared for the sick, worked in the fields, watered the donkey, expressed human affection, and were often raised to God in prayer.

What do you think of when you think of Mary's Assumption? I don't know why, but I always think of the hem of her dress; a dress that was doubtless as simple as a worn T-shirt and faded jeans would be to us today. I see its frayed, homespun cloth brighten as she is taken into the light of heaven. I want to see her feet. I always look for them under there.

I am sure that in the mysterious process of the glorification of her body, Mary's calloused feet were much honored in heaven; every scratch, each leathery sole, becoming what they always were — beautiful, heavenly bright. Maybe that's what happens in heaven. Things begin to look the way they look to God.

Come to Mary's House

You find her sweeping up her kitchen. She's pleased to see you, stopping to have a look at you. The sun from a window shines in from behind her, making a beautiful outline of gold around Mary. Notice a few things about her now — maybe the color of her dress, her eyes, her smile. What about her stands out to you today? Enjoy this moment. Then hear the swishing sound of her broom again. Maybe you should get the dustpan for her.

6
Mary Is Our Homegirl

*"A great sign appeared in Heaven: a woman clothed
with the sun, with the moon under her feet and a
crown of stars on her head. She was pregnant and
cried out in pain as she labored to give birth."*

— Revelation 12:1–2

Thinking of my own mother's dirty little feet when she came in from the garden, tracking mud on the kitchen floor, convinces me that Our Lady tracked dirt all the way to her son's throne. She brought the earth with her, I'm sure of that.

We are a very incarnational people, we Catholics. Earth is good, the body is good, because God is good, and Jesus is true God and true man — incarnate in the flesh. In spite of the airbrushed holy cards of Mary, in which her pupils seem far too small, and she is painted to look like a pastel ghost, we know that the stars in Mary's hair represent the way she looked to God — gloriously human, the humble and hardworking spouse of the Holy Spirit, who was lowly and invisible to the world but brilliantly radiant to the Lord.

Then again, our exalted Mother, as brightly shining as we see her in Revelation 12, shows us she is real and totally human. Even as heavenly Queen, rather than sighing with celestial bliss, she wails in the pangs of birth. That particular wailing is for us, I think. She is with us in our struggle with evil, in our determination to follow her Son, in our attempts and failures at practicing virtue, in the Church's painful war against the powers and principalities of darkness.

There is a trail of glory that Mary leaves, but it looks a lot more like dirty footprints to me, as she runs to the Seat of Mercy with our burdens and pains — with her requests for us, her lost, suffering, fighting, and dying children whom she wants to lead to her Son. Jesus, I like to think, must smile when he sees those clods of soil in the throne room that show she has been there. She will keep working for the kingdom until her work of Queenly discipleship is done, and there are stars in our hair too, as we reign with God forever.

Mary was assumed into heaven, body and soul. She is the living Ark of the New Covenant. She is Mother of God, Mother of the Church, the mother and sister of each one of us. She listens with a real heart, and leads us to Christ with real love.

The Assumption reminds me of this: Mary is real. She's tracking in dirt. She's holding my hand. And she's beautiful — the way God sees beauty. Not only that, but as Bishop Mike Sis said once in a homily, "The Assumption means God's gonna win! God's gonna WIN!"

In answering my Methodist friend, Paula, with an explanation of what the Assumption is, she exclaimed, "OH! Isn't that what happens in the end to all of us?"

Can I get a "heaven yeah!"?

Come to Mary's House

It takes a long time to get to her house today. Notice details along the way. Feel the earth under your feet, the sun on your skin. Here you are at last. She is just coming in from some work outside, washing her hands and face. She wants to start dinner, but don't let her do a thing! She's so tired. Ask her to sit. Gather a bowl, a pitcher of water, a towel. Take off her sandals. Wash her tired feet. Notice some small details about each of her feet as you do so. If you feel moved to, sing her a song, maybe a Marian hymn that you love.

7
Mary, Our Help

Remember, O most gracious Virgin Mary, that never was it known that anyone who fled to thy protection, implored thy help, or sought thine intercession was left unaided … I fly unto thee.

— Memorare

Sometimes I long for Mary like Jesus must have when he was away, especially when the disciples misunderstood him. I bet sometimes he just wanted to go home to her. At times I get busy like Joseph did in the shop, and I miss her. It seems nothing is right until I can find her and get a big hug from her.

When I am discouraged or my feelings are hurt, even the smell of her house can comfort me. And then she looks at me, her face blooming like a rose to see me, and I have to laugh at least a little. I gave up wondering how she could love me so much a long time ago. She just does. She loves you like that too.

Mary prays for you always. When she prays for you, her prayers make her present in your life. She is not a distant intercessor. She moves in. She puts the coffee on; she looks in your pantry to see what she can make a good soup out of. She clears the table, fills the sink with soapy water, grabs a broom, bandages your broken heart, listens to you, prays over you, calls her Son with updates.

If you feel far from God because of emptiness, anger, or pain, she will gently help you reconnect with him when you are ready. There is no situation she can't make at least a little bit better by her presence, by her compassion, by her prayers to Jesus for us. Place all of your burdens in her kerchief, and let her arrange them just so. She will tie them carefully, carrying them close to her heart, and showing them to her Son who will attend closely and affectionately, all the more in hearing your name from her.

So if you are troubled, run to Mary and be ready, because she comes "with haste," wind in her hair, and veil askew, to tend to you with the pure, strong love of a sister, a mother, a friend. Jesus is never far behind her. With her you see him in a whole new way — perhaps a deeper, more intimate, comfortable way. I don't know how she does that. I told you she is a sneak.

Come to Mary's House

She is sewing by the window, folds of cloth draped over her knees. She stops to get you a cup of something soothing and fragrant to drink. She waits for you to speak. Tell her everything that scares you, all that causes you grief, the most devastating, and even the smallest things. She listens carefully. Now she takes up the sewing she had been doing when you came in. She has been making Jesus a beautiful new robe. As you watch her needle making its strong, even stitches, you realize that somehow all that you have told her is being sewn into the hem of his garment.

M. Mashalei

8
Immaculate Heart of Mary

Mary, give me your Heart: so beautiful, so pure, so immaculate;
your Heart so full of love and humility, that I may be able to
receive Jesus in the Bread of Life and love Him as you love Him.

— St. Teresa of Calcutta
Commencement speech in 1982 at Niagara University

We often see images of Mary's Immaculate Heart, and we love them. They are pretty, and they remind us of Mary's love and purity of heart. Jesus said, "Blessed are the pure in heart, / for they shall see God" (Mt 5:8) because when we are pure of heart, all we see is God. Our eyes are opened as the space within us widens for the Lord, and we experience him everywhere, in everything, in everyone, and in ourselves, at all times.

Mary's habit of meditation in her heart would have made

her open and receptive to seeing God's angel at the Annunciation, and it would have made her able to hear and respond to his word. Her foundation in the love of God brought her to say, "Here I am!" (Lk 1:26–38). How can we imitate Mary within our hearts? We are so often unlike her inside ourselves. Sometimes we seem hopelessly off track. Our hearts long to be purified, to be cleared of all obstructions to seeing God, of all that holds us back from being able to love selflessly, be free, and run lightly in his paths.

We long to pray deeply and freely, like an oil poured out for Jesus. As it turns out, prayer itself is our way to purity of heart. Along with living a sacramental life and keeping a good conscience, prayer is deeply purifying. Prayer takes us to the depths where the Spirit can shine his light and truth, helping us to shed all that we must, making us humble, opening the way to union with God. We can grow (and glow) in Mary's spirit. We can cultivate her free and open heart to see God in all things, and be more and more receptive to his call.

As St. Lawrence Justinian said, "Imitate [Mary,] O faithful soul. Enter into the deep recesses of your heart so that you may be purified spiritually and cleansed from your sins. The acceptable offering of the spiritual purification is accomplished not in a man-made temple but in the recesses of the heart where the Lord Jesus freely enters."

If we persevere in prayer and intentional consciousness of God, we will find we have taken on aspects of Mary's personality. We will become more and more attentive to his Word in our lives. We'll learn to be in silent communion with him in the quiet of our hearts, as we become more and more aware of his indwelling, as Mary was. This awareness naturally flows into our relationships with the world around us. We'll experience a new openness and love toward people. We'll notice we are touching even inanimate objects with gratitude, even with gentleness and love. We'll feel a new clarity of heart. It may even seem as if God is drawing all of life to us along with himself.

This involves training ourselves to be quiet, to be recollected. It takes commitment to spend time with God every day in whatever way we are capable of, and to be persistent in prayer, striving always to live in God's presence. We can entrust our formation to Mary.

Come to Mary's House

When you come in today, Mary looks up quickly, her expression urging silence and caution. She nods toward her knee where a small dove is perched. She is trying not to disturb the little thing, so you take the nearest seat as slowly

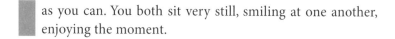 as you can. You both sit very still, smiling at one another, enjoying the moment.

9
Our Lady of Chayil

The woman of chayil, where is she to be found?
She is more precious than any jewel.

— Proverbs 31:10

The Hebrew word *chayil*, used here in Proverbs, is often trans-lated as "virtue." That's so boring, though, because *chayil* also refers — in other parts of the Bible — to warriors and armies, bravery and strength. It means someone of unusual courage, someone who is a fighter, a soldier for God (see Jgs 6:12, 20:46; 1 Sm 9:1a; 1 Chr 5:18; Ez 37:3–6, 10).

Who is a woman of *chayil*? Mary, of course, and she was *chayil* from the inside out.

I imagine that Mary would have had an inner solidity of trust in God, even regarding her own person; a trust that allowed her to rest in herself, with total holy confidence, as a child has rest in her mother's arms.

At the same time, this allowed her the detachment from self that made her humble and free to love in God rather than to love in a self-centered way. She operated from a strong foundation of love. She loved with the complete trust of a child and with the boldness of a warrior.

Mary's boldness of faith and self-possession first shows itself in Scripture when she questions the angel Gabriel about how this conception is going to happen, given her virginity, which she seems to think is a permanent state. (That's what she has to be referring to, otherwise the question makes no sense for a legally betrothed bride to ask. The angel had not told her when this conception would occur!) Once she understood how it would come about — as wild and glorious as she undoubtedly found it — she consented to God's vision with a committed daring of faith that we look back on with pride and awe. She is all in! "May the word you have given be fulfilled in me," she says (Lk 1:38).

We know that women who committed adultery were to be stoned to death (see Jn 7:53–8:11). Mary knew that was a risk given her inexplicable pregnancy. Such courage! With *chayil*, she leaves right away to visit Elizabeth, to bring the joy of Jesus to her, to be coconspirators with God together, and to be of help to her kinswoman in a time of need.

The Gospel of Luke (1:39–56) does not mention that anyone went with Mary on this trip. This is surprising, given that women were expected to be chaperoned, and it would have been dangerous for a young girl to travel alone. However, off she went! She didn't waste any time, either.

Nine months later, on the verge of delivering her first child, she loyally stays at Joseph's side to travel to Bethlehem. She gives birth in a stable, far away from the support of the women in her family and female neighbors who would have come to help her in her labor. Through her life she would:

- Flee to Egypt as a refugee
- Raise a divine Son
- Bear the loss of her beloved husband
- Follow her Son as a disciple
- Face a jeering crowd and Roman soldiers to remain at her Son's execution
- Be united in spirit with her Son, in the midst of the apparent defeat of everything she had known thus far with him
- Stay with the disciples who feared for their lives
- Experience the Resurrection

- Watch her Son ascend into heaven
- Experience the descent of the Holy Spirit at Pentecost with the disciples
- Begin life anew in Jerusalem with the community of believers
- Journey to Ephesus with John to begin yet another new life, far from anyone else she knew, for the sake of the Church

All of her life, she put the Gospel first, Jesus and his mission first, and love first. Her trust in God and her love of God were absolute and immediate, less like the submission of a servant and more like the impetuous, loving embrace of a daughter every time the Father's will was made known to her.

I think the secret of Mary's *chayil* was her love and her complete trust. She believed what the angel said: "the Lord is with you" (Lk 1:28). With this kind of faith God makes us brave and sets us free, even from ourselves, to walk ahead in courage, to leap, to dare for Jesus with the *chayil* of Mary.

Come to Mary's House

It's so cold out, and you're relieved to take off all of your winter layers and have some of Mary's hot soup. It's delicious.

You can feel it warming your whole body, all the way to your fingers and toes. She asks, "What is this worry you wanted to talk about?" Hmm. Maybe it is something in the soup she made you, but you can't remember all the things you were worried about before. It's a strange feeling not to be worried about anything. She wants to talk about living the Gospel completely and following Jesus without compromise, and she is talking about you. Strangely, you're not even freaked out. "More soup?" she asks. When you leave, she presses leftovers into your hands.

10
The Rosary

The memories of Jesus, impressed upon [Mary's] heart, were always with her, leading her to reflect on the various moments of her life at her Son's side. In a way those memories were to be the "rosary" which she recited uninterruptedly throughout her earthly life.

— Pope St. John Paul II
Rosarium Virginis Mariae, 11

The Rosary at its best is, to me, an intimate sharing between ourselves and Mary, as she invites us into our own family mysteries — the events in the life of Jesus. She intensifies our experience of the treasures of the Gospel by her presence, unique perspective, and teaching.

As Spouse of the Holy Spirit, she is an unpredictable, creative genius. She makes the Gospel new, real, and alive without us knowing how it happened. God is within us and — as Saint Teresa of Ávila points out in *The Way of Perfection* — that indwelling of God in us means that also within us is all his holy court, and all of heaven. Everyone in heaven is right here, in the "Little Heaven" of our souls.

Saint Teresa called the way of prayer "The Royal Road." Similar to today, there used to be a lot of roads people had to pay to travel on. But the Royal Road was free and open to everyone. This can certainly be said about the Rosary. It is a prayer for everyone, no matter what style or level of prayer each person who prays it is most proficient with. It is imaginative prayer. It is mental, interior prayer. It can lift us and become, if the Lord wills it, the mysterious grace of contemplative prayer that brings us into the deepest consciousness of God.

This Royal Road of the Rosary has been well trod by many before us, and there are fellow "rosarians" on this road any time we step onto it — people all over the world, praying the Rosary at any given moment, walking with us in spirit.

When I am about to begin the Rosary, I try first to quiet my heart, laying all my troubles and distractions at the feet of Mary. Then I pray to the Holy Spirit that I will be able to pray it well. If we want to pray the Rosary more deeply, it will take time. Mary wants our time. She wants to hang out with us. We want to hang out with her, too, without rushing. When we take time to really be with

Mary, she reciprocates, and our prayer is immeasurably deepened.

Sometimes we will be too overcome by anxiety or pain to pray in the usual ways, and the best we can do is simply hold the rosary, like holding our mother's hand. That is okay, too. As with any friend, there are all kinds of days with Mary. The important thing is to continue to live with her, rosary in hand, in faith, hope, and love, through it all.

Come to Mary's House

She invites you into her room today. She wants to show you the little murals she has painted over the years with homemade paint on the walls. Delighted, you ponder over several of the pictures. She is grinning over your shoulder, reaching out to touch a wonderful image of Jesus teaching with his arms wide. She guides you to other scenes, touching them, chuckling at some of them, because of memories of her own.

You are surprised to find a painting of yourself with Jesus. Maybe you say, "Hey that's me!" and she smiles. Some scenes show you as part of the Gospel story, as if you had been there. Other pictures you recognize as your own life, the vignettes showing Jesus taking part. In some of these, it is hard to tell which story is which. Choose one of these pictures to ponder, perhaps to ask Mary about.

11
Touching Base with Mary Through the Day

When Mary has struck her roots in a soul, she produces
there marvels of grace, which she alone can produce, because
she alone is the fruitful Virgin who never has had, and
never will have, her equal in purity and in fruitfulness.

— St. Louis De Montfort
True Devotion to Mary

As part of my commitment as a Discalced Carmelite Secular, I am to do something each day to honor Mary. It's easy when you love her! Here are some things to try in order to weave contact with Mary into your everyday, that she may "strike root" in your soul. Even just one of these will make a difference in your life for the better.

In her wisdom, the Church gives us three particular opportunities to check in with Mary at certain times during the day, that we might come to her in spirit. One of my favorites is the Angelus. This prayer is traditionally recited at 6:00 a.m., noon, and 6:00 p.m., to honor the Incarnation and Mary's consent (see Lk 1:26–38). The Angelus grew out of a twelfth-century tradition of praying three "Hail Marys" with the evening bell in churches and monasteries. Later, Scripture verses were added between the Hail Marys, along with a brief closing prayer. The Angelus also came to be prayed in the morning and afternoon in addition to each evening. (During the Easter Season, the Angelus is temporarily replaced with the Regina Coeli.)

I love thinking about how I am tuning in with everyone else who is praying the Angelus at the same time. I pray it at noon every day if I can. If not, I at least touch my forehead to Mary's in greeting for a moment in my heart.

The Magnificat (Lk 1:46–55) — Mary's song of praise — is recited with Evening Prayer in the Liturgy of the Hours. Even if you don't pray the Liturgy of the Hours, praying the Magnificat is a great way to share in Mary's joyful song and her celebration of the coming of the kingdom. After a while you will memorize it. Say it with her in the evening. It's good with a nice cup of herbal tea. Make one for Mary, too.

Night Prayer from the Liturgy of the Hours ends with an antiphon to Mary, such as the Hail Holy Queen. I think of it as our goodnight kiss to our mother as we go off to bed.

If you would like to start your day with Mary, something as simple as repeating her name a few times, or an Ave Maria, or another short prayer before you get out of bed, can bring a smile to your face and hers.

You might like to pray the Rosary each day or attend to other Marian devotions of your own, making them a part of your daily prayer life. I consider my brown scapular to be a constant, wordless devotion to Mary, and I often kiss it as I go about my day. I'm sure you already have, or can, come up with little ways to keep contact with Mary, too, that will be meaningful between you and her.

You can always make use of opportunities throughout the day to speak to her or remember her, as if you are experiencing the day and the people in it side by side with Mary. A simple movement of your heart toward her suffices, or a smile to yourself knowing she is near. She loves that.

Come to Mary's House

You don't find her at first, but she is hurrying around outside with everyone else. She explains, while still running, that since the sky is red and overcast, it means a big storm is coming. All the animals must be put up quickly. She has to chase chickens and get the stubborn donkey and the dogs in safely. Every time either of you catches a chicken, or one of the dogs, or makes progress with the donkey, you stop to high five. No matter what, she always has time for you! And you have time for her. Even if it is just a high five on a crazy day!

12

She Saw Who She Was in God

I thank you, because I am fearfully, wonderfully
made; all your works are wonderful!

— Psalm 139:14

In Mary's song of praise, the Magnificat (Lk 1:46–55), she says that the Lord has remembered her in her lowliness and that "from now on all generations will call me blessed." I am sure Mary needed the solitude of her journey to Ein Karem where Elizabeth and Zechariah lived, to try to process all that had happened. Can't you see Mary pondering her exchange with the angel, word for word in her heart, as it glowed in her soul? Perhaps the Holy Spirit opened the Scriptures for her along the way — as Jesus would do for the disciples on the road to Emmaus — to enlighten her understanding.

On nights she stopped to attempt sleep, she must have looked at the array of stars in the sky, and thought of Abraham. "Then the Lord brought [Abram] outside and said to him, 'Look up at the sky, and count the stars if you can. Your descendants will be like that" (Gn 15:5).

"Sarah must have come to mind for Mary as well. "God also said to Abraham, 'As for Sarai your wife, you are no longer to call her Sarai; her name will be Sarah (Queen). I will bless her and will surely give you a son by her. I will bless her so that she will be the mother of nations; kings of peoples will come from her" (Gn 17:15–16).

Maybe Mary had an insight that those stars represented her children, too. "All generations will call me blessed! The Almighty has done great things for me and holy is his name!" (Lk 1:48b–49)."

She is in awe, and she can scarcely absorb the role to which she has been called. As St. Thomas of Villanova said, "She is amazed at her own glory, nor can she herself understand her elevation" (Sermon on the Birth of Mary). As with any true gift from God, this amazement would only have deepened her humility. Saint Teresa teaches us that humility is just the truth about ourselves. Holy humility sets us free and makes us courageous. Humility that comes from the Holy Spirit should feel light and joyful, opening the heart. We understand that we are little, dust in fact, and it's okay. Humility gives us space to see ourselves as God does and also to behold our own wonderful mystery.

When we see ourselves in God's eyes, his yoke becomes easy and his burden, even the cross, becomes light. He shows us who we are to him, and we are filled with all that we need for the next steps of our journey. Perhaps we can go forward after all, when the path is daunting, once we know who we are in the Lord, doing all things in him who strengthens us.

Maybe, even, we shine with glory from the inside as we make our way through the elements of this world, with our eyes fixed on him whom we radiate.

Maybe this is how it was for Mary.

Come to Mary's House

Jesus is here. Mary takes your hand, leading you to the table where he sits. You feel shy, staring into your cup, but Mary gently puts her hands on your shoulders. "Look at him," she coaxes. You do. And you are captivated utterly by the beauty of his face, the dark loveliness of his eyes, the gentle tenderness and joy of his smile, the silent fire of his gaze, that comes from who he is, and from his love for you.

See yourself reflected in the pupils of his eyes. Call him by the name you most love to call him. Ask him this question: "Who do you say that I am?" Allow him, now, to speak to your heart.

13
The Visitation

Oil and perfume gladden the heart; so does the
sweetness of friendship comfort the soul.

— Proverbs 27:9

At the Visitation, Elizabeth repeats Gabriel's greeting — because she recognizes Mary as Queen Mother — and calls her "Mother of my Lord." Elizabeth confirms Mary in her mission by her own humble words of wonder, joy, and encouragement, filled with the Holy Spirit. Mary responds with her song of the Gospel that we call the Magnificat (Lk 1:39–56).

What must have passed between these earliest Church Mothers, these prophetesses, kinswomen, and friends, during Mary's three-month stay at Elizabeth and Zechariah's house? I imagine that these three months were a lovely weaving, as in the lives and friendships of many women, of daily work, love, and prayer. Maybe for them it was dishes and divine secrets, cooking and singing psalms, sewing baby clothes, drawing water, feeding the animals, tending the fire, breath-catching prophecy, washing and folding, praying and cleaning, laughing and crying.

Maybe Elizabeth gave Mary tips on morning sickness before the household recited the *Sh'ma* (see Dt 6:4). Perhaps there were harmless jokes about the speechless Zechariah. What did they think when they went to Synagogue on the Sabbath, knowing what only they knew? I imagine they pondered the Scriptures, pulled weeds, and planted seeds. They must have encouraged one another. What was it like in their quiet moments?

Did they stargaze at night in humble awe, overcome yet again with the mercy, greatness, and faithfulness of God, amazed at the ancient promise he was fulfilling in their persons? How astounding it must have felt that it was them in the midst of it all, at the epicenter of this secret new beginning for humanity.

How they must have grown in faith, love, and determination in the presence of the Holy Spirit in their relationship — theirs being the first Christ-centered friendship, a prototype of the Church. What did they talk about as they swept the floor, watched the sunset, and walked with the silent Zechariah after dinner?

Mary was most likely present at the birth of John the Baptist, along with the female neighbors who would have come to help. It seems she would have stayed for the circumcision and naming ceremony (Lk 1:57–80) as well. Did she stand in awe beside Elizabeth and witness the return of Zechariah's speech with his own wonderful, prophetic song? I bet she did. When Elizabeth watched Mary go, I wonder if she prayed the start of the Hail Mary again, to accompany the younger woman on her way, to lift her up in prayer as she went home to face all that she had to face, and to do all that she had to do.

I think of my friends, my soul sisters, who love, confirm, walk with, and encourage one another every day in our own Christ-centered relationships. Through them I have often known the Holy Spirit's presence and confirmation, love, and strength. I have thought, many times over the years, that there is nothing more beautiful to me than their faces at prayer, than being in the midst of their love, their work, as they transform the world around them. I would not be myself without their friendship. I would have become someone else.

I think of my friendship with Mary and how it has changed my life beyond recognition. And I have to say a Hail Mary. Because I love my life!

Come to Mary's House

You have been invited to share a meal with Mary, Elizabeth, and Zechariah. It is a joyous occasion, and after dinner Mary and Elizabeth are so happy they begin singing and clapping. Zechariah smiles and joins in by slapping his knees in time. They all stand up to dance, showing you the steps. Four steps forward, a little change of feet, four steps back. There is a lot of raising of the arms, clapping, and turning around. Enjoy the happiness, the togetherness, the joy of the coming of Jesus to a people who had waited so long, so long for him.

M. Mashaki.

14
Joseph

The Virgin, weighed with the Word of God, comes
down the road: if only you'll shelter her.

— St. John of the Cross
Romances 8

J oseph took Mary into his home. As a lover of God, he left behind his former thoughts and plans, as well as any fears he may
have had, to protect Mary and take care of her. He kept her by his
side always, no matter what anybody thought.

In all of the many challenges he and Mary faced, Joseph acted with daring in the service of the Lord and his Mother, every
time. We don't have any words of Joseph. Perhaps this is to em-
phasize the receptive quality of his soul to every indication of the
Father's will. He not only heard God's message in silence, but he
acted on it, dedicating his life to God's plan of salvation with im-

mense courage and leaps of faith. Saint Teresa of Ávila called Joseph a master of prayer. He lived continually in Jesus and Mary's presence, his life a beautiful practice of the presence of God.

Mary and Joseph would have shared a deep spiritual unity. After a day of hard work, it's easy to imagine them staying up late discussing the things of God. Maybe Joseph talked to her about what he and the other men were studying in the Torah. They would have prayed together in silence and simplicity, drawing their strength from God. As Jesus grew, they would have spent evenings listening to him and praying with him.

When Joseph died, he died in the arms of Jesus and Mary, in the midst of their prayers for him, surrounded by their love. Isn't everything that Joseph lived exactly what we want? We want to take Mary into the home of our hearts. We want friendship with her, to partner with her in her heavenly work. We want her to be real to us, to be someone we live with and have coffee with in the morning, someone to love Jesus with, work with, talk to all day, and kiss goodnight.

Joseph and Mary were the most in touch with the Sacred Humanity of Jesus — which, as St. Teresa emphasized, is our way to him. For many years, they alone knew the secret of his origin, speaking of it only with one another. Joseph was Mary's soul mate.

Mary loves to talk about Joseph. Her face lights up every time he is brought up. Whenever she goes to a party, people say, "Where's Joseph?" He is just getting her a cup of wine. He is always there. On the way home with Jesus asleep on his shoulder, they talk about how heavy he is getting, and how close they are to his revelation, wondering what it will be like, and exactly when it will happen.

Saint Teresa said that "whoever is attached to prayer" should seek out Joseph. In his quiet way, he will invite us into the family and teach us what he knows.

Come to Mary's House

Joseph has been working late in the shop. He washes his face, hands, and arms on the porch before coming inside. When he sees you, he says, "Stay for supper!" After giving him a big hug, Mary lays out dinner. Jesus spills his milk immediately. Joseph says the blessings, the meal is eaten, lively conversation is enjoyed. After dinner, as the lamps burn low, Joseph takes a scrap out of his pocket and reads a passage of Scripture. As Mary does, you sit in silence as you listen, ruffling the little Jesus' curls. He has fallen asleep in your lap. All of you fall silent. Feel the prayer of Mary and Joseph deepening your own. Listen to the breath of the little one, and breathe along with him.

15
Mary Rooted in Community

How good and delightful it is to live together as brothers! It is like precious oil poured on the head, running down on the beard, running down on the beard of Aaron, down upon the collar of his robes.

— Psalm 133:1

The home of Mary, Joseph, and Jesus would have been part of a compound of extended family, a group of houses and other buildings surrounding a courtyard where children played, and various work was done. The family would have farmed together to make ends meet. There would have been people in and out of their home during the day to help or be helped, to borrow something, to check in, to talk. Kids would have run through the house, into the courtyard, and into an aunt's house, perhaps.

Mary would have shared work, childcare, and elder care with the other women and stood with them at synagogue. She would have helped deliver their babies alongside her sisters, aunts, and cousins, sat at the bedsides of their sick and dying, walked to the well or to the market with them, shared news, recipes, and marriage advice.

She was part of her hometown also as "Joachim's daughter" (her father's name according to tradition). Mary would have been a sister, cousin, niece, aunt, sister-in-law, and friend. She was part of the life of her community, and she was important to others as they were important to her.

To grow spiritually we need one another. Even the original hermits of Mount Carmel were a community of hermits who attended Mass together, worked, ate, and prayed together, and met together to discuss various issues and plans. Catholic prayers usually begin with "Our" and "We." We ask blessings and help for "us" much more often than for "me." We approach God not only as individuals but as a community.

We receive Jesus in the Eucharist not just as ourselves but in communion with the whole Church. Mary understands how important this is. As a mother, there is hardly anything she loves more than seeing her children around the table of her Son, all of them getting along, loving one another, sharing their lives, fed by the same Lord, and one in him.

Mary was, as each of us is, a human being in community. Her life with God was inseparable from her life of love and relationships. By the time of Jesus' death, she had joined the Jerusalem community of believers, leaving her home to live among them full-time, as a mother and a sister of the disciples.

In union with the community of the Trinity, and all of the kingdom of heaven, she lives and works among us, drawing us into union with her Son and all of our brothers and sisters. Because where two or three are gathered in his name, there is he, and together we are his Bride.

Come to Mary's House

She wants to show you something. Leading you through the house and out the back door, you find yourself in a lush garden, laced with flowers and fruit. There are roses of every kind, trees, vines, and a spring that feeds it all. "My garden," she says. She shows you how the plants benefit one another, how the trees and the roses have entwined roots that help each other. Even after one of them dies, their remaining roots remain helpful to all. Together, you plant a new rose. Bless it with her. Now say to it, "Fulfill your holy purpose in this garden, take part in its life, be sacred to the Virgin." She smiles and squeezes your shoulder.

16
Hear with Mary the Cries of the World

Make your heart open, then the floods of that divine
love will flow into [your heart,] making it overflow
and bear fruit to the furthest reaches of the earth.

— St. Teresa Benedicta of the Cross

With a Marian perspective, intercessory prayer deepens and broadens to become a form of listening. Mary listens to the cries of the world right now, and her hearing becomes her prayer in the presence of her Son. At the wedding at Cana, she only had to see the distress of the families of the bride and groom, understand the situation, and then run to Jesus (see Jn 2:1–12) to be their advocate.

We can imitate her listening heart, and we can join her in

prayer as we experience and take in the day's events. We can be intentionally aware of God's presence, one with Mary's heart, rather than just seeing or hearing on our own without spiritual engagement.

How is this done? Have you ever had something sad from the news stay with you, being unable to stop thinking about it, asking God to send healing to all involved? Have you ever felt you had nothing to say to ease someone's sorrow, but prayed in silent communion with Jesus as you sat with him or her and listened?

When you did these things, you opened a door in your heart, and heaven came through. It touched everyone. Isn't that what Mary's life exemplifies? She hears and responds in a way that gives the world to Jesus and Jesus to the world. This is for us to do, too. In your own prayer, since we are all connected, you can be as present as she is to anyone, anywhere, especially in her company.

Mary can help us develop the spiritual dimension of the everyday experience of witnessing the troubles of the people around us, and of those we hear about around the world. We are still going to react emotionally to the suffering of others. Praying is not a way to escape the piercing of our own hearts, and we don't want that. We always want to grow in compassion.

Union with Mary's heart is empowering, though, because we know our tears have become a blessing for those who grieve. In this way, our sorrow or anger can be transformed into a spiritual fire that changes hearts.

In our prayer with her, Mary will take us all over the world in the wind of the Spirit — walking through the closed doors of human hearts, bringing the sweet breath of peace, calling others forth, urging them to "do whatever [Jesus] tells you."

In prayerful union with Mary, we will be led in spirit and nourished in heart. We will be enabled to caress the faces of those who suffer and ease their sorrows. In our own lives, we will respond to each person and situation from a mysterious reserve of inner freedom, courage, and love as we grow in union with Christ.

Come to Mary's House

There is, in the present day, a wall at what is thought to be Mary's house in Ephesus, built for her by John the Apostle. Pilgrims from all over the world attach their prayers and petitions to it. It is more than a wall with prayers on it — it represents the world and the cries of humanity. Walk along this wall behind Mary, touching a multitude of these ribbons and papers as you pass them, just as she does, until you begin to see people, Mary leading you among them. Watch Mary, help like Mary; listen closely to each heart, whisper encouragement to each soul. Pray to Jesus for them.

17

Pondering in the Cell of the Heart

Each one of you is to stay in his own cell or nearby, pondering the Lord's law day and night and keeping watch in prayer unless attending to some other duty.

— *Rule of Saint Albert* #10

It's not hard to imagine the early Carmelites — "the Brothers of Our Lady of Mount Carmel" — being inspired by Mary, their spiritual sister, to live a simple life built around prayer, as she had done while on earth.

While these men on Mount Carmel lived as hermits who gathered for Mass or for meetings or meals only at certain times of the day, Mary, as we know, was immersed in family life. I think Mary, amongst her family, would have been centered in the cell of her heart, where she could "ponder the law of God day and night." The early Carmelites built a community life that reflected Mary's continual consciousness of God within, withdrawing to pray in the secret of their cells where they could be alone with God.

How would Mary have pondered Scripture? Women in Mary's time were not taught to read. However, it is clear that Mary knew a lot of Scripture (the Magnificat is full of Scripture references, especially to the song of Hannah, mother of Samuel, found in 1 Samuel 2:1–10). Some of the friars among the first Carmelites were illiterate as well. Still, they pondered the law of God from Scripture.

The Bible was read aloud at meals, while the friars ate in silence. They also heard God's word at Mass daily. And perhaps in the Marian spirit, and similar to the Desert Fathers and Mothers before them, they spent a lot of time memorizing Scripture, committing the words to heart as they heard them so that they might pray and meditate with them as Luke's Gospel tells us Mary did in close proximity to the Word himself.

The first Carmelites strove to pray without ceasing — "keeping watch in prayer" —identifying profoundly with Mary and with the Prophet Elijah and his disciples who had lived there before themselves.

In the cell of our hearts, then, in the presence of the Lord who lives at its center, "We meditate on your unfailing love, O God" (Ps 48:9), with Mary, who "treasured all these words and continually pondered over them in her heart" (Lk 2:19).

Come to Mary's House

Settling down with Mary, the two of you chat about the day. After a while she brings up the Prophet Elijah and seems to enjoy retelling you the story of the "still small voice" of God that Elijah heard and recognized (1 Kgs 19:11–13). You notice that she touches her heart lightly as she speaks, the way a pregnant woman touches her belly now and then. She leans over and touches your heart, too. You understand. The two of you drop into silent prayer.

18
The Silent Witness of Carmel at Fátima

Let Mary's soul be in each of you.

— Saint Ambrose
Commentary on Luke

During the final apparition of Fátima, Mary appeared briefly in the brown habit of Carmel, as "Our Lady of Mount Carmel," a silent witness to Carmelite spirituality and the order's unique relationship with her.

The appearance of Mary as Our Lady of Mount Carmel at Fátima may indicate that the devotion to her Immaculate Heart encouraged at Fátima is, on the deepest level, about having our hearts do what the Gospel of Luke says Mary's heart did: pondered the life of Jesus, the Word of God, in her heart (see Lk 2:19).

The charism of Carmel is exactly that: intimate prayer, meeting God deep in the heart, pondering the word of God day and night, in deep harmony with Mary, seeking fruitful union with God for the sake of all.

The three shepherd children who saw Our Lady at Fátima said the light from Mary's hands made them, "See ourselves in God more clearly than in any mirror." This experience sounds like the true and holy self-knowledge that is one of the fruits of contemplative prayer, which is Carmel's focus.

At times, the crowds at Fátima felt a cooling wind in the heat of the day. The sun dimmed, to the point that the people could see the stars. Flower petals rained gently down. As a Carmelite soul, that imagery enchants me. I think of the breath of the Holy Spirit that draws the soul away from the weary world to the inner life of prayer.

Eventually even spiritual consolation will fade, as the soul quests deeply for God, and discovers the stars of faith that can only be found in the night of the spirit. "The soul subsists purely on faith," says St. John of the Cross. Then, in a kind of rebirth, the secret blessings of union with God rain down silently on the soul — now so much like Mary's own — until it can say, as did St. Elizabeth of the Trinity, "He is my Heaven!"

Now, more than 100 years after Fátima, perhaps it is time — as the beauty of Carmel has taught us — to be the medicine that heals the world. To quote Saint Thérèse, "In the heart of the Church, my Mother, I will be love" (*Story of a Soul*, chapter 9).

So pray like a Carmelite. Pray. Until prayer becomes love, and love becomes prayer. That is the activity of Mary's immaculate, simple, and beautiful human heart, which Carmel seeks to imitate for Jesus and for the salvation of all the world.

Come to Mary's House

She is working on a frame loom leaning against the wall. She doesn't look up, but she smiles when you come in. Sitting on the floor beside her, you look at and touch her weaving, taking in all of its lovely shades of rich brown. She stops to measure your shoulders, nodding to herself as she returns to her work. Stay and watch her as she weaves.

M.Mashalei

19
Mary and Lectio Divina

Mary heard the Word of God and cherished it in her heart.

— Antiphon from the Liturgy of the Hours
Memorial of Our Lady of the Rosary

Lectio divina (which is Latin for "Divine Reading") involves reflectively reading a passage of the Bible (*lectio*) and pondering a word or phrase that has stood out to us until we receive light on what God is saying in our souls through that word or phrase (*meditatio*). Then we respond back to God in prayer (*oratio*) and then rest in his love in communion with him (*contemplatio*). Finally, we take action on the fruits of the prayer (*actio*).

If you think about it, Mary could be seen as *lectio divina* incarnate. Her life was one beautiful flow of all of the steps of this prayer. She received the Word of God (*lectio*), nurturing him in herself — in her body and in her heart (*meditatio* and *con-*

templatio). She sang out her praise response in her Magnificat (*oratio*). She then brought forth the Word-made-Flesh into the world, caring for him as mother (*actio*). She continued to do this throughout her entire lived experience with Jesus, reflecting on each event, each word, in her heart. To every sign of God's will she responded generously.

When a woman shouts out to Jesus from the crowd, "Blessed is the womb that bore you, and the breasts that nursed you!" (Lk 11:27), he answers, "Rather, blessed are those who hear the word of God and keep it." As I interpret this, Jesus means that to see Mary as a holy vessel, as being blessed merely because she is his biological mother (as the woman in the crowd seems to imply), is to dismiss the Mother of the Word and what she is here to teach us by her life and being. "I would rather you do what she has done. Hear the word of God and keep it!"

Jesus also told us that we can and should do all he is doing (see Jn 14:12) and, in this, he seems to also include what Mary has done and is doing. She received every seed of the Gospel with joy, planting it in the good soil of her heart where it bore fruit a hundredfold (Mt 13:8). She gave all, and so she received all; in good measure, overflowing, shaken down to make room for even more, poured into the hem of [her] garment (Lk 6:38). We know that Mary was blessed, that all generations would repeat that truth (Lk 1:42; 48b–49).

There is a saying that Mary "never keeps anything for herself." She shares her bounty with you! And she takes you to Jesus to drink more deeply of his love than you otherwise could, because her soul magnifies the Lord (Lk 1:46).

When we pray with Mary, she guides us in quiet, hidden ways, bringing us into a more vivid prayer infused with her knowledge and love of Jesus. We don't just call her blessed. We become what she is. We, too, are the mother, the sister, the brother, of Jesus, and of Mary, when we treasure his word and keep it.

Come to Mary's House

You are at the kitchen table with Mary, reading aloud the Mass readings of the day from the Bible and drinking coffee. You see she takes in each phrase that stands out to her, repeats it, and pauses to consider, so you do the same. What are you reading? Ask questions, perhaps exchange thoughts with Mary, as the two of you read over again what you have read. The Scriptures seem particularly alive to you today. You both fall into silent prayer. Flowers begin to grow out of the pages, touching your faces. They smell amazing.

20
Searching for Jesus in Faith

Rejoice in your hope . . . be patient in trials and pray constantly.

— Romans 12:12

Even though Our Lady possessed extraordinary grace, she relied on faith in her daily life and in the midst of events that challenged her. This is comforting because faith is accessible to all of us. We only know of angel messages for sure once in her life. Think of the three days Jesus was lost to her as a child (see Lk 2:41–52). Mary had no visions and Joseph dreamed no dreams. They had to seek their Son in faith, just as we do.

There are times in our lives when God doesn't seem to hear us, and things are not okay. We have to trust that God understands what is happening, even though we do not. Perhaps our outward lives are going well enough, but we feel we have somehow lost Jesus. We no longer sense his presence or feel any delight in prayer. We're bereft. We're dismayed. We retrace our steps, call his name in all of the places we were with him before, but we cannot find him.

Mary and Joseph had the singular opportunity to enjoy the physical presence of Jesus daily, to listen to his voice, live with him, care for him, and embrace him, until he slipped away without them knowing, just as they were on their way home from faithful observance of the Passover.

They were good, holy people of faithful observance, and still Jesus left them.

With intensifying concern, they sought their Treasure in distress until he was found. When they saw him, he seemed different, giving them an answer they didn't quite understand. We too must persevere. Whatever happens, we continue to seek Jesus our Treasure diligently, faithful in prayer.

When we catch up to the Beloved, we too find him a bit different. This may be because, as we grow, we also have to grow our image and understanding of God. He is continually revealing himself to us in new ways we have to make room for. We must find our footing with him again; our prayer has changed.

We rally from our surprise at him and simply take him home with us once again. His presence seems to grow in us then, and we are closer to reaching our "full stature in Christ" (Eph 4:13).

At the same time, we must know he is always where he is supposed to be. He is here in the temple of our hearts all the time, doing the Father's work. Now we're ready for anything. Mary was.

Come to Mary's House

It's cold and dark inside. As you bump into one piece of furniture and then another, you realize it has all been rearranged. So you stand where you are, calling Mary's name. You hear her footsteps near, and you strain to see, perceiving only the slightest outline of her form. She opens her cloak to drape it over you. Just before it settles over your shoulders, you glimpse the universe — stars, galaxies, and planets, glittering underneath, an unfathomable depth. Then you're in darkness again, but feeling Mary's warmth. She is leading you somewhere. Ask her where you are going. What does she say? Where does she take you?

21
With Us in Our Work

Mary counts your steps and your labors.

— St. Maryam of Jesus Crucified
Maryam: The Little Arab, Amédée Bruno, SCJ

We should try to avoid the idea that work takes us away from our prayer or gets in the way of our spiritual lives. Admittedly, it's hard not to feel that way at times, especially when we are just getting the hang of praying and being with Jesus, experiencing his presence within us.

Mary had so much to do, too. Undoubtedly, she took that awareness of the Lord's indwelling into all that she did.

So, as St. Teresa of Ávila, Brother Lawrence (a seventeenth-century Carmelite friar), and Saint Thérèse teach us, we will find the Lord with us in the midst of our work. As Saint Teresa says, "The Lord moves among the pots and pans" (*The Book* of Foundations).

Prayer, especially once we are well grounded in it, begins to flow out into our lives and actions.

Saint Thérèse taught the novices at her convent to make the beds as well as they could, as if they were making them for the Holy Family. Mary was always doing all she did for Joseph and Jesus. So we are definitely in good company with Mary when we do all we do around the house, or at work, as if it is for the Holy Family, or if we are conscious of our work as a gift to the ones God has given us to love in our lives.

Brother Lawrence says, "We can do little things for God; I turn the cake that is frying on the pan for love of him, and that done, if there is nothing else to call me, I prostrate myself in worship before him, who has given me grace to work; afterwards I rise happier than a king" (*The Practice of the Presence of God*).

We know from the "Little Flower," Saint Thérèse, and so many other guides in the spiritual life, that when we are rooted in Christ, he makes our smallest acts of service or sacrifice reverberate throughout the world for the good of all souls, just as he does with our prayer. All that we do for him he expands into a mystery of grace in union with all that he himself has done — all of his love, the immensity of his sacrifice, and his healing power are shared with us in this way. We become co-redeemers with Christ, as Mary was in her deep sharing and offering of the sacrifice of his life that God has made incomparably fruitful.

As a Jewish woman, Mary would have prayed all day as she worked. She would have touched the *mezuzah* and then kissed her hand when she came into the house, to remind herself of the truth and the presence of the Lord and her love for him. She would have been responsible for the family's faithfulness to Jewish dietary laws as a way to honor God. With her prayerful awareness of this, I am sure she made the experience of cooking and serving food an offering beautiful to him. She would have prayed over the bread she made, the work she did, her Son's play, and as she lit the evening lamps, the prayerful duty of the woman of the house.

When we concentrate on our necessary tasks, this draws us into the moment, and the moment is where God lives. We can make those moments a silent meeting place. Reflecting the soul of Mary, we can consecrate our chores and acts of service throughout the day. God will touch each one with his glory. We can do this by a simple gesture or movement of our hearts as we begin and carry out our tasks. Heaven will receive our wobbly, often distracted offerings with all of our mixed motivations and feelings, as precious in God's sight through Mary's hands. She will say to Jesus, "Aww! Look at this one!"

Come to Mary's House

When you come in, Mary is busy cleaning, scrubbing her house. She hands you a bucket of water so you can help. Out of the corner of your eye you see her lift her scrub brush with a soft smile as if it were an offering to God. You try this too. How does it feel?

22
Deep Repetition

[Mary] the name of that beautiful flower which I
always invoke, morning and evening, drew my entire
soul and reminded me of the greater focus.

— Dante Alighieri
The Divine Comedy: Paradise

One of my favorite spiritual books (tattered and taped together on my shelf) is the two-part work titled *The Way of the Pilgrim* and *The Pilgrim Continues His Way*. It is the story of a Russian peasant and his spiritual growth as he wanders through Russia, learning to pray without ceasing by repeating the Jesus Prayer ("Lord Jesus Christ, Son of God, have mercy on me, a sinner"). Initially, he uses the Jesus Prayer as his way of communing with Christ in mental prayer (what is called "Prayer of the Heart" in the Russian Orthodox tradition) each time he stops to rest. In time, he discovers that his heart continues the prayer no matter what he is doing, without effort or interruption, becoming a constant impulse of his heart toward God. Throughout the book, the Pilgrim details how love and consciousness of Christ grow in his heart along his way.

Another work from an anonymous author, titled *The Cloud of Unknowing*, is from the Middle Ages. It talks about how a word of love to God, like a spark, pierces the "cloud of unknowing" in which he resides, taking us out of our tendency to try to grasp toward God ineffectually with our intellects, and instead bringing us straight to his heart, far past places the mind can go.

One of the ways I keep close to Jesus and Mary through the day is the simple praying of their names. When I am doing a task that doesn't require a lot of thinking, I repeat the names of Jesus and Mary. This helps me drop my preoccupations and brings me into conscious awareness and attentiveness to the presence of God. It is also a prayer because I am calling on them in my heart and in this way dedicating whatever I am doing to their love.

Doing this in the waiting times of our lives can bring us into focus as well, so we can fill those empty spaces with the Lord — at red lights, between tasks, waiting for water to boil, walking somewhere. It is very helpful in times of stress, anger, or fear — anytime we need to recenter. I have prayed it silently at times

I was doing my best to remain present to someone who was suffering overwhelmingly. At those times, the Holy Name of Jesus and the sweet name of Mary kept my heart open to listen deeply and give what was needed.

Try saying Jesus' and Mary's names a few times when you first wake up. See how that feels to you. You could work on getting in the habit of saying them as you fall asleep, to take them with you into the night.

St. Rose of Lima is said to have memorized the names and titles of God from the Bible during a time of blankness and darkness in her prayer life, and she repeated them while she did her embroidery or any task that allowed it. It was her light through that difficult time.

Saint Francis repeated, sometimes all night long, "My God and my all." I love St. Joan of Arc, and I love that her banner said, "Jesus. Maria." So, years ago, I began saying this silently and often. I say it whenever I remember to — "Jesus. Maria."

It's easy for me to imagine that, once the Angel Gabriel had revealed to Mary the name of Jesus, she would have silently repeated it often, day and night. And what would Joseph have thought of with each heartbeat and each step but, "Jesus. Mary. Jesus. Mary."

Come to Mary's House

She is outside working with her family, helping with the plowing. You can smell the turned earth, the scent of hard-working animals and people. Mary smiles at you, tools in hand. Together you follow the plow, raking up weeds and grass left behind, tossing them into a pile. The work seems to go on and on, but Mary's presence, laughter, and occasional singing lift your spirits. She hands you a bag of wheat berries to sling over your shoulder. Go with her, scattering seed, scattering seed, scattering seed.

M. Mashafei

23

The Way of Spiritual Childhood with Mary

*Truly I say to you, anyone who will not receive the
kingdom of God like a child will not enter it.*

— Mark 10:15

Every November 21, the reflective heart of the Church presents
to us the quiet marking of a minor memorial — Mary's pre-
sentation at the Temple as a small child. It is a story that was first
recounted in the Protoevangelium of James, a second-century
noncanonical gospel that recounts Mary's early life. She was danc-
ing, the story says, up the Temple steps when she was dedicated by
her parents to the Lord. Even the solemn old priests had to smile
as they watched her, this girl who, unknown to them, would one
day teach the Messiah his prayers.

It doesn't matter whether this very old story about Mary happened or not. It's true, anyway. This memorial was given to us by the Church for a reason. It points us to who Mary is and what she did in her life. In this ancient snapshot, we can see a baby picture of our own Christian souls, with a child's pure heart, free for God. Mary is our mother and sister. Her life reflects our lives and spiritual developments as we grow in Christ.

My friend, Fr. Gregory Ross, OCD, says that St. Thérèse of the Child Jesus, who gave us the "Little Way" of spiritual childhood, was "like a little Virgin Mary." Pope Francis, speaking of Mary at the Annunciation, remarks, "She recognizes that she is small before God and she is happy to be so" (Angelus, December 24, 2017).

The "Little Way," as Thérèse called it, is about great confidence, love of God, a joyful humility, and acceptance of whatever life gives with a spirit of offering. It is distinguished by spiritual freedom, simplicity of heart, and a bold, childlike faith. Mary kept her pure, open heart as a humble and small — yet greatly loved — daughter of God all of her life, in both trials and joy.

Maybe we can remember little Mary and try to think of ourselves as the littlest children of God, striving to be enthusiastic and free of heart. Maybe we should try to grow down instead of up. We could carry this picture of Our Lady's childhood close to our hearts — that we may remember who we are and where we are going, that we might enter the kingdom of God in the same way she ran up those steps, and be what the little child Mary was that day: tender, bold, brave, joyful, and bright with love. If the kingdom is within us, why not start now? Ready, set . . . GO! Last one up is a rotten egg!

Come to Mary's House

Her mother tells you she is playing outside as you come in. Here she is, building a tiny house of pebbles and wildflowers. A warm wind lifts little Mary's hair when she turns to look at you, pulling it away from her face as she smiles. You squat down, becoming even with her littleness. She reaches over and clears your own tousled hair from your face, peering at you closely. She walks away a few steps, then turns to beckon to you. "Come on, dis way," and she begins to run. Follow her!

24

Our Lady of Mental Prayer

God is spirit, and his worshipers must worship in spirit and truth.

— John 4:24

The primary devotion to Mary in Carmel, according to Fr. Aloysius Deeney, OCD, is meditation, or mental prayer, which is the practice of silent interior prayer (see his work *Welcome to the Secular Order of Discalced Carmelites*).

It makes sense that Our Lady would be most honored by us loving her Son the way she did every day — by our loving presence to him. Reflecting her devotion, we treasure Jesus within us. Deeply receptive to the Holy Spirit, we meditate within our hearts. All of these things are exemplified in the life of beautiful Mary. Though it may sound esoteric, in actuality the practice is simple and humble and grounded, like Mary herself. Mental prayer is an intimate conversation with the Lord, filled with friendly silences, yet holding hidden glory. As St. Teresa of Ávila says, "Mental prayer is nothing less than taking time to be alone with the One who we know loves us" (*The Book of Her Life*).

The Lord is overwhelmingly generous. It is mysteriously fruitful to take even a few minutes each day to be receptive to the "secret, quiet and peaceful inflow of God" (St. John of the Cross, in a letter to a Carmelite nun). Our prayer is made mystically far-reaching by God. Like Mary, when we meditate and pray, we become channels of God's love and grace, of his holy will.

The praying soul is like a window opening — sunshine and a warm, sweet wind flow through that soul to everyone and everything. Its clear openness fills the whole world, and each of its situations, with healing light. The rushing wind and brightness of the hidden spirit of prayer changes hearts, lifts up those who suffer, and makes a way for peace to happen. It sets people and all of life free.

We are so little, but it is God who draws us to prayer. In his creative power, because of his joy in sharing his divinity with us, and because of the Incarnation of the Lord in the marriage of humanity with God, the smallest breath of prayer suffuses the universe in a flow of light and beauty. In the beginning, the Spirit of the Lord breathed upon the waters, and life sprang from his command. Jesus walked among us, re-creating, redeeming, and renewing the world by his life, by his death, and best of all by his resurrection. We are baptized into union with him, infused with his love.

He could have renewed the world by himself. But he shares his mission with the littlest of us because of his love. He has lifted us up to join him in his creative and redemptive work. I think this is what it means to "reign with Christ."

In prayer, living water has come to gush from our hearts, watering the earth around us and even in faraway places. So give yourself to prayer without a doubt in your mind. We don't always know what God will do. But we know he will do something. Just open the window of your soul as best you can, letting God do the rest. Mary invited us to do this when she said, at the wedding at Cana, "Do whatever he tells you" (Jn 2:5).

Come to Mary's House

She brings you a cup of tea and you fall into conversation. She begins telling you stories of Jesus, and you enjoy watching the joy on her face as she does. What is she telling you? Eventually she says, "Let's pray," touching you lightly. You grow still and quiet. Pray together with Mary a slow, attentive Our Father. She gives your hand a little squeeze.

25
Mary's Hidden Beauty

The kingdom of heaven is like treasure hidden in a field.
When a man found it, he hid it again, and then in his joy
went and sold all he had and bought that field. Again,
the kingdom of heaven is like a merchant looking for
fine pearls. When he found one of great value, he went
away and sold everything he had and bought it.

— Matthew 13:44–46

I'm following her through the house as she brings in the laundry. As she leans over her basket, a handful of jewels fall out of her hair. I'm not sure she saw them. I've noticed this with her. Flowers open as she passes but no one sees, least of all her. Only God knows Mary's hidden beauty. Sometimes he gives hints like these of what she means to him. I begin to help her with the folding. Smiling to myself, I fish some of the colorful gems from among the robes, rugs, and curtains, holding them close to my heart.

At the perfect time, Mary's precious, pure humanity was conceived in human love in the womb of her mother, Anne. So much about Mary is hidden but exceedingly beautiful. Her glory was like a pearl in a shell — God's own secret of what was to come, his quiet mystery veiled in the dark silence of the womb. Already, she was in the perfect innocence of the first Eve. Already, she was in communion with God without impediments. She was innocent beyond all innocence then in existence. She was already completely full of grace. The King of the Universe must have loved looking at her, the private jewel of his heart, unassuming and humble in the world, but to heaven clothed with light. Her glory was like an unseen star shining on all humanity.

But she was not luminous to anyone but the Lord, and all of her queenly jewels, her beautiful starry crown, were only for the angels to smile at as they watched her pad around the village on her errands, laugh with her friends, sweat in the fields, ponder the word of God in her heart, carry water, wipe Jesus' nose, or burn the lentils.

In the world she lived in, she was just a Jewish girl, of low socio-economic status, of the peasant class, in a small, Roman occupied territory at a time of violence, oppression, and political upheaval. She lived a life of hard work (approximately ten hours of hard labor per day, for most women in her situation), few rights, and a seemingly constricted future. To the world of her day, as in the countries many girls are born into still, she would have been seen as of less value than a son — and, as a Jew, of less value than the Roman occupiers. But in the eyes of God, she was the beautiful field in which he would one day hide the Treasure that was and is his own Son.

And what about you? Don't you also hold the Pearl of Great Price, the Treasure, within you? Aren't you a little Mary in this world?

Come to Mary's House

You see that she is in prayer when you come in, so you close the door softly and take your place to pray beside her as quietly as you can. Right away you can almost sense her prayer deepening yours. Stillness comes at once when you are with her. It would be hard even to come up with any words or thoughts of prayer now. The silence and stillness become full, and everything else disappears to you but Jesus and the peaceful love he awakens in your soul. Something falls lightly into your lap. It's a pearl.

26
Incognito

She cooperates with a mother's love [in the generation and formation of the faithful].

— *Lumen Gentium*, 63

Upset after a big fight with my mom and brother, I was walking super quickly across town to my dad's house. It was cold, and I had forgotten a jacket. A car full of girls from school drove by, rolling their windows down to jeer and shout insults. I picked up a bottle to throw at them, satisfied when glass shattered hard against metal, and the car drove away, leaving me in silence.

I stalked across campus (central to my college town), an angry sob rising in my chest. I remember leaves blowing across the wide, concrete spaces between buildings. No one was around as it was almost Christmas. Even the fountains were off.

It was a long walk to my dad's, but my anger propelled me.

When a pretty, smiling girl came riding up and hopped off her bike, I was surprised and exasperated. When she asked if she could talk to me, and said she really felt God led her to talk to me, I just wanted to put my face in my hands. Raised without religion in my small Texas town, I was used to being "talked to." Sometimes I felt trapped and embarrassed, sometimes offended. I did know the best thing was to attempt to be polite and get it over with.

So I told her she could talk to me if she wanted. She started pushing her bike alongside me. We must have made a funny pair — a young, smiling woman with bouncy brown hair, in a pink ski jacket, jeans, and white running shoes, pushing her bicycle beside a miserable looking teenage girl in ripped up jeans (not as acceptable then as they are now), a homemade punk T-shirt, and a beret over her shaved head.

The girl asked about my life; what I had been doing. I found myself telling her this and that, nothing dramatic. I noticed she seemed sad at times as I spoke to her, and I wondered why.

She said she had a message for me from God, that God wanted me to know he loved me. She said God wanted to warn me that my life ahead was going to be a very hard one, but that he would be with me. (On all of these counts, I realized several years later, she had been correct.)

"You don't have to follow God in the same way everyone else does," she went on. God wanted me to know that was okay. "You can believe in God in your own way." The girl in the pink ski jacket asked if she could hug me. "I just really want to, is that okay?" I let her hug me. She said she loved me. ("Um, okay.") I realized I hadn't asked her name. "Mary," she smiled. I remember her shy shrug in the sunshine.

We had both just turned around to go our own ways when I thought to thank her, since I knew she meant well, and turned right back an instant later. There was no one there, wherever I looked in that wide, open space. Until ten years later, when I had a dream about riding bikes with Mary, I didn't realize what this experience had meant.

Come to Mary's House

She meets you along your way, walking back with you toward the house. Sit on the porch with her and chat. Today, ask Mary where and when she has been with you and intervened for you in your life. Be receptive. What does she say to you? Continue your receptivity after your prayer time, be attuned to what happens around you. Similar to her Son, she often speaks through the events, songs, conversations, and things we read in daily life as well as in our solitary prayer. Don't forget to thank her with all of your heart for all that she has done for you.

27

Do You Want to Live?

Oh, all you who suffer, come to Mary, at the
feet of Mary, I found life again.

— St. Maryam of Jesus Crucified
Maryam: The Little Arab, Amédée Bruno, SCJ

I was lying in the middle of a busy intersection. It was night. People were running to and away from me. I watched their feet. There was a gentle glow growing in the corner of my vision. This light was communicating to me. Even though I didn't "believe in God," there was no question to me then that this glow was God, and that God was asking a question.

"Do you want to die now?"

I thought about it. "I don't know. I'm not sure," I answered honestly.

"Okay. Think about it. I will come back later and ask again."

When the EMTs arrived, I was able to give my parents' names and addresses, say what day it was (March 24, 1984), answer who was president (Reagan), and tell my name and how old I was (16). At the hospital sometime later, I overheard my parents' conversations with the ER doctor. Later this would surprise them, because they had been in another room from me.

I had been hit by a car as I crossed Texas Avenue on foot at night. I had been waiting to cross, but I had decided to go ahead because of impatience and because I didn't care for my life anymore. My pelvis was crushed, my right ankle and wrist broken, my neck sprained. I had internal bleeding. I had been thrown ninety-two feet in all, with a bounce in between.

I was staring hard at a boring painting of bluebonnets at the end of my hospital bed, struggling to deal with the pain (I had not been given pain medication yet), when I realized that there was a woman, veiled and draped in black, holding a rosary and praying incessantly beside my IV pole. I had no idea what she was saying. I tried to stay awake for her, but I kept passing out. After what seemed like hours, she stopped and stood silent. I couldn't think of a polite thing to say to her. I finally said, "That was a very nice prayer. Did you make that up yourself?" No answer. I lost consciousness again.

Later, I asked about her. Nobody knew about whom I could

possibly be talking. After that, God came back. The bluebonnet painting disappeared, and a quiet light came through the wall, asking, "Have you thought about it? What did you decide?"

"Yes. I've decided I want to live."

"Are you sure? If you live, your life will be very difficult, very hard."

"I want to live. I want to be strong, like my granny, and live."

"Then you will live."

Whatever is happening with you, God is with you. Your relationship with God is unique and precious to him. He has been with you at every turn, always allowing you to choose, and following your steps with love. He has sent his mother to be with you, to pray over you when you have needed her, to pray that you might choose life. God has come to you with gentle love and asked you, with an open hand and an accepting heart, "Do you want to live?"

(Strangely, this experience did not convert me for more than its duration to a permanent or active belief in God. I filed it away, not knowing what to do with it. However, the Holy Spirit brought it to mind at the right time for me when I was ready.)

Come to Mary's House

Today, Mary wants to pray over you. Let her. She has taken your hands in hers and closed her eyes to begin. Be still, be open. You may wish to kneel, or to sit quietly.

28
Mary Elaborates

He has filled the hungry with good things
and sent the rich away empty.

— Luke 1:53

That line of the Blessed Mother's Magnificat used to bother me. It sounds mean. I have often asked her what she meant by it exactly. I love the joyful way she has answered in my life. Years ago, my daughters and I had an eccentric, flamboyant, and charming homeless friend named, let's say, "Joe." We talked to him when we saw him and tried to help whenever we could.

One hot day, I was on my way to my brother's house with my two kids in the backseat — Máire, then eight years old, and Róise, only four. They were not being particularly well-behaved in the back of the car. I got a call from Joe. I said, "Hey! How are you?"

He said, "HOT! I'm very hungry and thirsty. Do you have any change so I can eat and drink?" He sounded hoarse.

"Where are you?" I asked. He was about a block away. All I had was a twenty-dollar bill for the week. I thought about it. I had paid the bills and gotten groceries for the week. But if I gave Joe the twenty, as I wanted to do, if we ran out of bread or milk, we would have to wait until payday for it. I was willing, I decided. I would be fine. Joe needed it more.

I headed his way. "Where are we going?" asked Máire.

"We are going to help Jesus out today. He's hungry," I answered.

"He smells bad!" complained Róise from her car seat.

"Pretend he doesn't," I suggested.

"Stop being so rude, Doorknob!" Máire scolded her sister. "Just offer it up!"

We pulled into the McDonald's parking lot where Joe was waiting for us. I jumped out of the car and gave him a hug. The girls waved from the window. He waved back and asked them if they were being good today. This question they wisely declined to answer.

Joe wasn't looking too good. I was worried he might be dangerously overheated. He said he would be okay when he had something to drink. He was so happy about the twenty dollars, he practically danced! He was wearing what looked like a bull-fighter's outfit that day. A dance would have been perfect.

As we pulled away from a very happy and relieved Joe, who had been so hungry and now had the prospect of lunch and maybe even dinner, I looked around at my beaming, waving kids, and felt the smile on my own face, even though I was now broke for the week. Then I realized that the hungry had been filled and the rich sent away empty. But both were happy!

Come to Mary's House

She has been busy outside and is pleased to settle down in the kitchen and visit with you over a nice, cool drink. Is there anything you would like to ask Mary? Is there something she can clarify for you? Ask her and remain open to her answer, both now and as you go about your life.

M. Mashele.

29
Living Reparation

I am the Mother of the Poor, Mother of the Savior, Mother of God.

— Our Lady of Banneux

I have to kneel at Gloria's bedside since it is just a mattress on the floor. I gesture to the tub of soapy water. She nods solemnly, having already been consulted by her sons about this. Seeing her plight is deeply heart-wrenching to me. I am a caregiver. I am accustomed to bathing bed-bound people who are sick, disabled, or in pain. I have just never seen anything like her situation before. I bathe the swollen, arthritic hands of this emaciated woman, who has found no room, no help, no comfort among us in her time of need. I can't believe this happens to people. But I try to be as present as possible to her in a simple way, setting those thoughts aside. As a Christian aide, over time I have become attuned to the love of God present in these encounters, not just for the afflicted person, but for myself. It seems to me that the Holy Spirit lives and loves within these exchanges, and that Mary is involved in the process. Tasks like this can carry a sense of liturgy when experienced this way — every part of the task feels sacred.

As I work, it seems that the hands I bathe are holy to Mary. When I unzip Gloria's sweat jacket, Our Lady of Guadalupe's serene and prayerful face peeks out at me from her T-shirt, as the zipper goes down. Of course Mary is here and making her presence known. Gloria's rheumatoid arthritis has become unnecessarily advanced and irreversible due to poverty, fear arising from the mixed immigration status of her family, and lack of access to care. The pain must be unspeakable.

She and her kids have been living in one room they rent with the sixteen-year-old's meager pay from his afterschool job. The boys have cared for her on their own. Lately it has been impossible for her to bathe herself as her illness has progressed. She has been too embarrassed to allow her teenage sons to do so thus far. Her arms, which she can barely move because of the pain, have to be scrubbed for long want of attention. The skin is rough and cracked. I take off bright yellow socks from her twisted feet, being careful to wash between each crooked toe. She sighs with relief as I lay the hot washrag on her chest and stomach. I add lotion and a few dabs of lavender essential oil over most of her skin, with her permission.

We Catholics often make reparation to the hearts of Jesus and Mary for the disregard and insults of the world toward them. We intentionally love them in place of those who will not or cannot. It came to me as I worked with Gloria that perhaps this was what I was doing and experiencing — living reparation to their compassionate hearts for all that Gloria had suffered. After all, she is made in the image of God, and the world has walked by like the priest and the Levite in the Parable of the Good Samaritan (Lk 10:30–37).

With a growing sense of reverence, I wash her long, black hair. I wipe her face, trying to do so as tenderly as I would for that of my dearest child or my own mother — or the Mother of God herself. I start to feel peacefully happy, and think of this as a sign of the Holy Spirit's presence with us. I sit back on my heels wringing out my washcloth one more time. Gloria and I look at each other, both of us smiling as if we are about to laugh. I thank her for letting me help out. I know it was hard.

"Gracias, Chawn," she says.

"You're my Queen, Gloria," I say. "Mi Reina!"

She smiles. "Ok, Chawn." Bemused, she puts up with me. But I mean it.

Come to Mary's House

There are other people here today to see Mary, many have brought flowers, lit candles. But the Mother of Jesus only has eyes for their faces, and their tears, touching each one with tenderness. She has asked you to bring to her today someone you know of who is heavily burdened and suffering. When she sees you both, what does she say to you and to this dear person? What happens?

30
Annunciation House

*Truly your strength is not in numbers, nor your power
in strong men. But you are a God of the humble, the
defender of the little ones, the support of the weak,
protector of the abandoned, savior of those in despair.*

— Judith 9:11

The first thing I saw when I came through the screen door at Casa Vides was a large painting of Our Lady of Guadalupe and two women who looked very much like her sitting on a weathered couch, one with a newborn, the other with two broken ankles. I thought, "This place, too, is Mary's house."

I was in a migrant shelter in El Paso where I and several others would spend five days learning about border issues and taking part in the daily life of Casa Vides, one of several shelters of the Annunciation House network there. Most of the guests also resembled Mary in their socioeconomic status — they had lived lives of hard work in lands full of political turbulence and violence. As Mary had, many had fled with children to protect.

The women I met in the shelters we visited understood Mary's closeness to them. In one of the shelters, I saw a group of ladies meeting at day's end for prayers near her image, rosaries in hand, something they apparently did nightly.

On a quiet afternoon when I didn't go with the rest of my group into Jaurez, I saw the two women I had met the first day. The young widow with the newborn helped the one with broken ankles get out of her wheelchair and onto the couch. I plopped down across from them in front of the TV.

At one point, I got them a couple of water bottles from the kitchen. I wasn't sure they needed them, but they said "Sí," seeming to understand my need to do something for them, giving me encouraging smiles. We laughed together at the show we were watching, in spite of our language barrier. We greeted people coming in, and sometimes one of the Sisters joined us on the couch for a little while. It was a lovely afternoon.

During my stay, Our Lady of Guadalupe was ubiquitous, her portrait at every shelter and institution we visited. Notably, her image came up often in the art of the migrant children who had been held in Tornillo. One of the young artists had written alongside his image of her "God is here." I thought perhaps that was her message to him during that hard time.

Mary of Guadalupe's face was also everywhere at the Walmart shooting memorial, among the photos of the dead, prayers, poems, candles, flowers, and children's toys. She showed up, too, along the migrant-themed Stations of the Cross that we prayed as we trekked up Mount Cristo Rey to the altar and cross at the peak. She was everywhere we went. This was a message to me that she was very present with these migrants and refugees. I saw they felt she was among them in solidarity — an image of faith, hope, and love, and so they kept her image close.

Sometimes I felt helpless and outraged at the needless suffering they experienced. I asked one of the volunteers, who had committed to live at Casa Vides for two years, and who was impressively patient and kind, how he managed the anger and distress himself. He said it was hard, and sometimes he felt he couldn't do it anymore. But it had come to him that their migrant guests had such faith, and they were the ones who suffered these things. He thought that if they could have faith and carry on with hope, he could too. Their faith was impressive to me, too. No matter what had happened to them, they would say gravely at the end of their stories, as if to reassure their listeners, "God was with us."

In El Paso, I learned that Our Lady can be found in all of the places Our Lord said he himself could be found (Mt 25:31–46). She is there among the least of our brothers, among our sisters who suffer, caring for Jesus in them. As my daughter Máire put it when I told her about this, "She sees her Baby in every face." The mother of Jesus wants us to see him, too. And here will be our joy. I never noticed before that not only is Our Lady of Guadalupe pregnant, but her knee is slightly out to the side. I was told in El Paso that that is because she is getting ready to dance!

Come to Mary's House

There are a lot of people here today for dinner, laughing, talking, helping one another. You've been standing on the threshold watching. Just as you notice Jesus there at the table, a beaming Mary pulls you in.

31
The Strength to Be Still

More than all of them, their mother ought to be admired
and remembered. She saw her seven sons die in a single
day, but she endured it . . . because she trusted in the
Lord. Full of a noble sense of honor, she encouraged
each one of them in the words of their fathers.

— 2 Maccabees 7:20–21a

Mary remained still, even inside herself. She was still because she was listening for God, and she was occupied with his will — and, because of her love, she was completely present as the unthinkable happened to her Son. The Scripture says only that she was there (see Jn 19:25).

There was no way her instincts as a mother were not the strongest that could be. However, she did not attempt to stop anyone, scream at anyone, blame anyone, say anything, or do anything but stand as she watched her Son be tortured and murdered before her. Any parent would find this hard to imagine. Since we know she was an incomparable mother, we know this stillness was not wrong of her. It was right.

She chose to be still because she trusted Jesus, and she took her lead from him. She remained focused on him, and she let nothing get in her way. She would never let anyone steal her treasure — her union of heart and will with Jesus — no matter what was done to her heart and soul by what was done to him.

She faced everything, even this unbearable brutality, as it happened, not knowing the future. Nothing could stop her from loving and doing what was asked of her in the moment, even if it was to stand and be desolated. And that is strength, if that is what is right. And it was totally right.

In the stillness she kept, she was able to sense her call to ally herself completely with the offering of her Son and join him. Her silent strength and her courageous proximity to her condemned Son must have been a rare wonder to those standing by. She needed to remain completely present to him, loving him. She wanted to be totally open to God's purpose in this traumatic event as it unfolded in her life, no matter how horrific it seemed. She had to pay attention and keep watch with her Son, listening for the Holy Spirit, trusting the Father. She understood this, and nothing could stop her, not the hatred and mockery of the angry people around her, not the cold efficiency of the soldiers of Rome, not even her mother's heart crying out within her in the face of what she had to see and experience.

In the midst of all this, she was still. Such was her fierce focus and priority. She was neither passive nor weak. She was unbelievable.

Sometimes it's time to say, "Son, why have you done this to us?" and sometimes it is time to be silent, to be present, to be still. She knew how to respond or not respond, because she listened and she watched, and because "her heart could not want what God did not want" (*Diary of Saint Maria Faustina Kowalska: Divine Mercy in My Soul*) even when she lost everything, even God, her own Son.

Her response of stillness on Golgotha models for us the gospel meaning of turning the other cheek: I will not be turned back from love. Her eyes were on God. Incomparable Mother, incomparable disciple.

Come to Mary's House

She is sitting, silent, still, and grave on an empty workbench. Sit at her feet now. Feel all of your love for her. Keep your eyes on her and let her gaze at you, too. Repeat this phrase several times, slowly and reflectively, with love and respect, "Holy Mary. Holy Mother of God." A movement catches your eye. There is a large butterfly on her shoulder solemnly drying its wings. She doesn't notice it because she is resting her heart by looking at you, whom she loves very much.

32
Battle-scarred

To what can I liken you, that I may comfort you, Virgin Daughter Zion? Your wound is as deep as the sea. Who can heal you?

— Lamentations 2:13b

I have long been drawn to the image of Our Lady of Częstochowa. I love her dark skin, her piercing eyes. I especially love the scars on her face — slashes of the sword by a marauder long ago. I think these scars are an important message, and I have felt their power. So many of us are inwardly defaced to some extent — heavily scarred by sorrow, cruelty, violence, and tragedy of one kind or another. Mary, too, suffered profoundly.

The slashes on the cheek of the Black Madonna of Częstochowa remind me of how real and human her suffering was. And I need to know that about her. In our day we might say that Mary suffered from post-traumatic stress. I don't think this is outlandish or a denial of her spiritual status or the joy she knew in the resurrection of her Son.

I have no doubt his rising again was an incomparable joy. I am sure she experienced a profound, transforming love at Pentecost that helped her bear her Son's physical absence and deepened her understanding of what had happened. But I believe her scars remained. Even as she carried the brilliant light of the Gospel with deep happiness and peace, there were still the marks of the sword in her pierced heart.

After his resurrection, Jesus retained the wounds of crucifixion on his body. Mary's wounds were emotional and psychological. As long as she lived among us, I think she would have carried these. There would have been traces of this in her eyes.

Dealing with my own woundedness, and in the midst of every tragedy in my life, she has prayed with me, "Lord, increase the strength of my soul" (Ps 138:3). And God has given me what I needed to bear everything.

Saint Thérèse said to Jesus, "I want to love you like a little child, I want to battle like a warrior bold." Like so many things Thérèse said, I think this describes Mary's own life. When we love the Lord like a little child, being humble and small, knowing we are out of our own strength, we are able to let ourselves be loved, and he prepares our arms for war (see Ps 144), for the battle of earthly life. Those slashes on the cheek of the Virgin of Częstochowa do resemble war paint.

I think the wound of the sword in Our Lady's heart (see Lk 2:35) would not have become infected so that the wound would have bled cleanly. The thought of this has led me often to ask God that I not become bitter and unforgiving from the tragedies of my life, but that my heart, too, will bleed cleanly and become wiser, gentler, and more compassionate.

Of course, I would rather not have had to suffer as I have. I think Mary would rather not have, too. Jesus himself said, "Let this cup pass from me, but not my will but yours be done." Mary had to have had her moments, too. But when the time came, she paid the price of love with full commitment.

I made a series of pilgrimages during a time of crisis in my life years ago. I visited the Marian shrines around Texas. At the shrine of Our Lady of Częstochowa in San Antonio, and in the church of Our Lady of San Juan del Valle in San Juan, I felt gripped by a mysterious, very feminine power that was almost terrifying. I can only describe it as "dark," though it was not at all evil. Reflecting on this later, I thought that Mary had revealed the immensity of her strength and presence to me, and that sense of being spiritually gripped by her was her fierce embrace — the darkness, her mantle drawn over me. I needed that embrace so much. "Are you not in the crossing of my arms, are you not in the fold of my mantle?" she asked St. Juan Diego.

In the midst of blinding pain, Mary embraces us. There need be no lesson, no words, no romanticizing or philosophizing of our desolation or even its spiritual rewards. Mary, in all her reality, is simply there with us.

Come to Mary's House

Today bring symbols to Mary — a handful of small representations of your griefs. These are your *milagros*, traditionally left in shrines as tokens of petition. They are usually small, flat, tin representations of, say, a broken heart, a part of the body that is ill, a bottle representing someone's alcoholism, or a little figure of a child, perhaps. Start laying these out on Mary's kitchen table. Before you can finish, Mary has swiftly taken you into her arms. In her haste, some of the *milagros* are knocked to the floor by her sudden movement and the edge of her robe, along with some of the dishes and the lamp. You can smell that comforting Mary smell of her hair and clothes as she envelops you tightly in her strong arms. Stay, even if you become emotional, scared, or angry. Just stay.

33
Holy Saturday to Dawn

In the dark night of the soul, bright flows the river of God.

— St. John of the Cross, in a letter to a Carmelite nun

For the Son whom you merited to bear,
alleluia, has risen as he said, alleluia.

—Regina Coeli

She knew how to surrender herself completely; knew for a fact that her Son was divine. She had treasured every event of his life, every word of his teaching. She would surely have continued to do these things, even on that desolate Saturday after his death.

Mary was intimately connected to his purpose, and she persevered in this knowledge, even as she was plunged into the pure darkness of faith alone with no other inner light or spiritual sense, as abandoned in her soul as he had been on the cross.

Given who her Son was, she had to know this wasn't the end. Her Son was eternal. He had said he would rise on the third day. She held on to that. The disciples were confused about this, but to Mary understanding it wasn't the main point. She had been puzzled by pronouncements of her Son before, and she knew that the thing to do was to wait and see what God would do. Whatever it may be, or whenever the "third day" was, she was to trust and to accept, for however long God wanted, and to keep watch in prayer.

So she waited and she prayed. The disciples began to pray with her. Some needed a hug, or a word of forgiveness for running away, for being afraid. They were still afraid and devastated, lost. It was hard for her to speak, but she could touch a shoulder here, hold a hand there. She could cradle Mary Magdalene in her arms, the poor darling.

She cried with them and tried her best to be a tangible link to her Son and to the truth of all that he was. She knew the brutal images of the day before would run through her mind daily for the rest of her life. She also knew her rest was in loving, and this she did.

The holy women wanted to go to the tomb as soon as the

Sabbath was over to anoint the body. This was the work of the women of the family. They presented the herbs, flowers, and spices to her for her approval, but something about it didn't seem meaningful or right to Mary. Something about this anointing nagged at her. She knew that this was how they wanted to show their love, and she said it was alright. They were very surprised she didn't want to accompany them. It was her right to wash and anoint the body of her Son and rewrap him in his burial clothes.

Early in the morning, the women set out with the spices and all that they needed to perform this last service. She smiled gently at them and let them go. John was worried that she chose to stay, but she assured him she felt a little better. She had a little something to eat, washed her face and hands, brushed out her hair, tucked in some of the flowers he had brought her, and went out to watch the sunrise, and to wait.

She realized why she had not wanted to go to the tomb. Because . . . she was pretty sure Jesus wasn't there.

Now where was he?

The birds had woken up and were singing when Mary caught sight of Mary Magdalene running wildly in their direction.

A voice behind her, with a catch in it said, "Mom."

She turned.

Come to Mary's House

She runs out to greet you, flowers in her hair, wearing her wedding bracelets on her wrists, her face radiant with joy. "Guess who's here?" she asks you, pulling you inside.

34
Spouse of the Holy Spirit

The Holy Spirit will come upon you, and the power
of the Most High will overshadow you. So the holy
one to be born will be called the Son of God.

— Luke 1:35

What does it mean that Mary is called "Spouse of the Holy Spirit"? Is it because she conceived Jesus by the power of the Holy Spirit? Or is there more to this title the Church has given her that has some bearing on the destiny of our own souls?

What I think of when I call Mary "Spouse of the Holy Spirit" is the "mystical marriage" — the union of God with the soul — experienced by St. Teresa of Ávila, St. John of the Cross, St. Catherine of Siena, St. Rose of Lima, and other Christian mystics throughout history. The spirituality this engenders is called "Bride Mysticism."

We know that before the Fall, Adam and Eve walked in the Garden of Eden with God, speaking to him and presumably seeing him. Their fall from grace was tragic, but because of it, Jesus has come into the world. Now we will share in the divine life of the Trinity, to an even greater degree in heaven, beyond anything we have known or dreamed could be. This is a gift immeasurably more wonderful than that of Eden.

Mary, though she is the New Eve and without sin, still lived as our sister in our fallen world, living by faith as we do. We know that she was a lover of God. She would have sought God with all of her heart but without the impediments that often entangle us in fear of him, and without the need for purification we have. We know that God also sought her.

He loved her so much he wanted to marry her. And she said yes.

St. Teresa of Ávila said about "mystical marriage," "I make this comparison [of marriage] because there is none more suitable, [but] this secret union takes place in the innermost center of the soul where God Himself must dwell" (*The Interior Castle*, Seventh Mansions, chapter 2). This marriage happens through "the working of the Holy Spirit," she says.

With all tenderness, God came to her soul, and she gave him shelter. What was this like? Saint Teresa says:

So mysterious is the secret and so sublime the favor that
God thus bestows instantaneously on the soul, that it
feels a supreme delight, only to be described by saying
that our Lord vouchsafes for the moment to reveal to it
His own heavenly glory in a far more subtle way than
by any vision or spiritual delight. As far as can be understood, the soul, I mean the spirit of this soul, is made
one with God Who is Himself a spirit. . . . He has thus
deigned to unite Himself to His creature: He has bound
Himself to her as firmly as two human beings are joined
in wedlock and will never separate Himself from her.
(*The Interior Castle*)

So the two become one.

If spiritual marriage can happen by God's grace to human
beings who are open and receptive to it by the practice of prayer
and virtue, how much more so could it happen to the Blessed
Mother, as she took on her great mission as Mother of God. This
union is a transforming union, a union of the love and life of
God with the life of the soul.

Part of the experience of this marriage is a revelation of
the Trinity. Just think! That knowledge was completely new to
Mary! I don't think of this event as fiery or dramatic. I think it

would have happened like a breath, as simple and immediate, in the clarity of her soul as soon as she said, "I am the Lord's servant … May your word to me be fulfilled" (see Luke, chapter 1).

And where do you think you are going? The Church is the Bride of Christ, as is your own soul making her way to union with God: "As a young man marries a young woman, so will your Builder marry you; as a bridegroom rejoices in his bride, so will your God rejoice in you" (Is 62:5).

Come to Mary's House

You can hear her singing in her sweet, untrained voice, in another part of the house. You like listening to her, so you pause. It's a song about rain on the meadow, about buds bursting forth, something about an apple tree. Go and find her with a smile on your face.

35
To Dwell in Her Heart

I dwell in the heart of my Mother. There I find my Beloved.

— St. Maryam of Jesus Crucified
Maryam: The Little Arab, Amédée Bruno, SCJ

To me, to dwell in Mary's heart and to find the Beloved there — besides being enfolded in her love, and the fact that, of course, Jesus is in her heart — implies a kind of Marian mindfulness, a participation in Mary's way of being and loving God.

When Jesus was away in the desert or preaching, she went about her work in the garden, with her weaving, cooking, hauling water, kneading bread, caring for the animals, and talking with friends and family, in union with him. In all these events, he remained always with her spiritually, as much as when he lived in her womb or in the house with her for so many years. Now and then maybe she paused, raising her hands in prayer for her

Son, and for the whole world.

Mary kept her spirit close to his, as always, uniting herself with the mission of Jesus. God was with her, and she was with him. As with most prayer and spiritual progress, reaching this state takes a combination of discipline and grace. We all live in a river of thoughts — plans, dreams, memories, and worries, all day. Rather than be swept away, invite Jesus to step right into the current with you. Turn this river of thoughts into a continual conversation with God, as often as you can remember to, addressing your thoughts to him as often as you can in the spirit of Mary, and helped by your connection to her.

Brother Lawrence, a Lay Carmelite Brother, wrote about the "practice of the presence of God" in his book of the same name:

> He does not ask much of us, merely a thought of Him from time to time, a little act of adoration, sometimes to ask for His grace, sometimes to offer Him your sufferings, at other times to thank Him for the graces, past and present, He has bestowed on you, in the midst of your troubles to take solace in Him as often as you can. Lift up your heart to Him during your meals and in company; the least little remembrance will always be the most pleasing to Him. (*Practice of the Presence of God*)

As Saint Teresa of Ávila taught, we should imagine the Lord always with us and keep him company. When he sees we want to be with him, we will find he responds eagerly. Then, she says, we won't be able to get rid of him! More and more he will be there with us, making us smile at random times. It becomes not so much an effort as the way we are. Brother Lawrence writes:

> This practice of the presence of God, somewhat difficult in the beginning, when practiced faithfully, secretly brings about marvelous effects in the soul, draws down the abundance of God's grace upon it, and leads it imperceptibly to this simple awareness, to this loving view of God's presence everywhere, which is the holiest, the surest, the easiest, and the most efficacious form of prayer. (*Practice of the Presence of God*)

Come to Mary's House

How strange! She is wearing her wedding dress to do her daily work. Sensing you should say nothing about it just yet, taking her lead, you help her hang out laundry, grind grain, set the bread to rise, do the shopping. She acts normally, talks with friends, interacts with sellers. No one notices the wedding dress. She gives you a wink. What do you make of this? Following her to the well with the water jar, you notice you are wearing wedding clothes as well. Jesus is here, and she sneaks off, leaving you alone with him.

36
Mary's Heavenly Work

Show unto us the blessed fruit of thy womb, Jesus.

— Salve Regina

As Catholics, we know our work in the kingdom of God does not stop with our earthly deaths. We know we will "rest in peace" in the heart of the Blessed Trinity when we reach heaven. However, we will also take part in the life of the Trinity, which is never static. God is "Lover, Beloved, and Love," as Saint Augustine expressed (*De Trinitate*, VIII). In God's nature, there is constant activity, an outpouring of love and creativity.

When we who are made in God's image give our life to love, we see that it then spills over — it is always moving, going out, a cup overflowing. So will our eternal lives be. As all of creation yearns for the new heavens and new earth, the holy ones in heaven are very much involved in the process that God is working everywhere.

Both St. Thérèse of the Child Jesus and St. Elizabeth of the Trinity, two Carmelites who mirrored Mary so well in their souls and wore Our Lady's habit, were granted insight toward the end of their lives as to how they would serve the kingdom of heaven after their deaths. Saint Thérèse famously said, "Oh, I will come down! I shall spend my Heaven doing good on earth! I shall let fall a shower of roses!" (*Saint Therese of Lisieux: Her Last Conversations*, 62, 102). St. Elizabeth of the Trinity wrote that she would draw souls into union with God in prayer when she got to heaven, and begin her mission for us there (Letter 335).

We know heaven's Queen is even more active in our lives, in the life of the Church, and in the whole world than the other saints. Saint Thérèse, discovering her vocation as love, reasoned that if the Church is the Body of Christ, and we are all parts of it, then she would be in the heart. She would "be love in the heart of the Church" (*Story of a Soul*, chapter 9). Elaborating on this, my friend, Fr. Gregory Ross, OCD, says, "Who is love in the heart of the Church more than Mary?" Indeed.

Mary has been given unique power and love for our sakes, and for the sake of the kingdom. She has the gift of drawing souls into the embrace of her Son, gifts of healing, conversion, peace, protection, and victory over evil. When we hear Mary's greeting, we are stirred with a deep inner joy and filled with the

Holy Spirit. We begin to truly pray, drawn into the meditations of her heart. She spends her heavenly glory on us.

She is a midwife of souls born again in Christ. She is an evangelist and teacher of prayer.

There is so much more to Mary that we will be learning all of our lives. After our deaths, we will know and love her even more. However, Mary can never be enough for us. She isn't trying to be. As someone who loves us completely and knows exactly what we need, she wants us to have Everything, God himself, and she knows the way.

Come to Mary's House

She has left the door open today. You walk through the open house, savoring its peace. There is a well-worn path between her backdoor and the carpenter's shop. Mary has left a trail of rose petals the length of it, and so, smiling, you follow. There is Jesus. Let every thought fall from you like dust, settling gently into the wood shavings on the floor. Look at Jesus. Let him look at you. He brings a lamp from the windowsill to you. It begins to shine with every possible color. Together you hold this warm, beautiful light between you.

37
Building a Life of Prayer

Many and varied are the ways in which our saintly forefathers
laid down how everyone, whatever his station or the kind
of religious observance he has chosen, should live a life of
allegiance to Jesus Christ — how, pure in heart and stout in
conscience, he must be unswerving in the service of his Master.

— Rule of Saint Albert, #2

The nuns of the Teresian reform asked St. Teresa of Ávila to write about prayer for them. She responded with *The Way of Perfection*. Most of the book is not directly about prayer but about building a life of prayer. The *Rule of Saint Albert* is the way the first friars on Mount Carmel built their lives on the foundation of prayer.

In order to create a spiritual life in which we can devote ourselves to prayer and holy living, whatever our state in life, we need the space, interior and exterior, to pursue this, so that prayer permeates the whole of our lives. When Mary wanted to use herbs in the bread she was making, she would sprinkle a handful over the dough, kneading it in until every part of the loaf had herbs in it. So begin with a little handful, starting with something you think you can most easily make a habit of, and start kneading!

Ask Mary to help you be faithful to your humble commitment, and begin in her honor.

Dedicate to her a moment of quiet at a certain time each day, attaching it to something else you already do, such as your cup of coffee in the morning. Drink it with Mary. Resolve to clear your schedule at least a little, and to clear your mind and your conscience so that you are as unimpeded and as free as possible to follow the way of prayer with her.

Just as Mary's presence permeated the atmosphere of the early community of Carmel as the Lady of the Place, so her simplicity and groundedness will guide you into a rhythm of days of communion with God, leading you to "good works, my daughters, good works" (St. Teresa of Ávila, *The Interior Castle*).

If you are like me and your life is more like a jazz solo than a meticulous string quartet, it's okay. Everyone is different. Overplanning will make you feel constricted, and you will give up before long. A jazz solo needs a rhythm section to flow from, though, so put a few touch points in your day as a basis for your improvisation. If you are a string quartet, the structure of prayer will likely be easy for you. Only try to remember that this effort is about God and not about the plan itself, or you could overdo it and miss the point. You will enjoy making your own rule of life that works for you, and your music will charm heaven just as much. Whatever you do to begin, maintain your rhythm and grow in the spiritual life; do it in humility, littleness, and love as Mary did everything, and you will be doing well. The important thing is to keep kneading and keep up the music.

Come to Mary's House

You are teaching the child Mary how to play tic-tac-toe. She doesn't seem to understand the rules of the game though. Every time you draw an O, she throws herself into your arms. Each time you write an X, she covers your face with kisses.

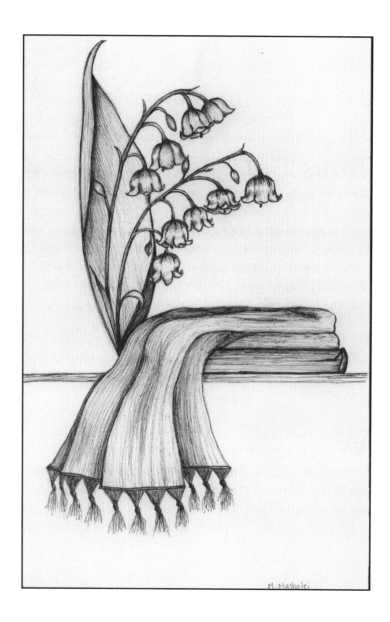

M. Mashalei

38
Totus Tuus

*Consecration to the Mother of God is a total gift of self,
for the whole of life and for all eternity; and a gift which
is not a mere formality or sentimentality, but effectual,
comprising the full intensity of the Christian life —
Marian life. [Marian Consecration] tends essentially
to union with Jesus, under the guidance of Mary.*

— Pope Pius XII
October 31, 1942, speech

What does it mean to consecrate ourselves to Mary? To me it is about seeking a union with her that leads me into the inmost heart of Jesus. The immediate fruit of my first consecration to Jesus through Mary, which I made with my first husband, was an intensified love for Christ in the Eucharist. Neither of us expected that at all. When we noticed this change in ourselves, we wondered what was happening. One day, we found ourselves simultaneously weeping at Mass when the Host was raised, filled with awe. We recommitted ourselves fervently to our holy Faith.

We eventually realized the changes we were seeing in ourselves were Mary's doing and stemmed from our consecration. She had brought the Holy Spirit with her, giving us clarity of heart, the fire of devotion, and awe in the presence of God.

The long-term fruits of Marian consecration in my life have been her leading me into a life of prayer, her Marian Little Way, Carmel, her love of Jesus, and her compassion. Over the years, I have renewed my consecration to Mary in different ways. Lately, it is as sister and friend that I am with her most often, my scapular a silent sign as I go about my day, and as I sleep at night.

Jesus said, "I do not call you servants any longer, because the servant does not know what the master is doing; but I have called you friends, because I have made known to you everything that I have heard from my Father" (Jn 15:15). Mary feels the same way. She invites you to a deeper bond with her, to join her in her heavenly work, to cherish Jesus within you and to bring him to the world, to make her concerns your own. She has so much to share with you. You are family. So come. Consecrate your beautiful Christian soul, your glorious Christian life, to Mary — to her heart, to her way — and watch your life bloom into all that the

Father dreams of for you.

How does one make a consecration to Mary? There are different ways, both traditional and new, available to you. The important thing is that your commitment and gift of self is done in a way that is the most meaningful between you and Mary. Maybe the simplest is the best: "I am completely yours, Mary, and all that I have is yours. I take you for my all. O Mary, give me your heart. In the Name of the Most Holy Trinity. Amen" (St. Louis De Montfort, *True Devotion to Mary*).

Come to Mary's House

A lovely meal is ready on the table, and a small altar has been set up with candles and flowers. Jesus is here in his best robe, and Mary looks her prettiest. Friends have gathered, people who love you best, living and dead. The saints you are closest to smile at you, gifts in hand. Jesus says you're looking wonderful and leads you to the altar near Mary. Jesus tells you that from now on, wherever Mary's heart is, your heart will be there beside it. With everyone singing your favorite Marian hymn, Mary hands Jesus a brown, woven cloth she has draped over her arm, and Jesus clothes you in it. She steps forward to adjust it; it's a woven brown work apron worn over your shoulders. It fits perfectly. Jesus hugs you.

Mary hugs you. Say to them the words of consecration. Turn to your friends. Receive their embraces, their gifts. All of you share the meal Mary has made.

39

Mother of the Church

Redeemed by reason of the merits of her Son and united to Him by a close and indissoluble tie, she is endowed with the high office and dignity of being the Mother of the Son of God, by which account she is also the beloved daughter of the Father and the temple of the Holy Spirit.

— Lumen Gentium, 53

There they are, those brilliant stars encircling her head as she turns to me when I come in. Even after the stars become invisible again, I'm in awe, filled with gratitude and love for her. What I want to do is fall to my knees at her feet, to take hold of and touch to my face the hem of her long blue skirt. But I can tell she doesn't want me to do this. What she really wants is some help in the kitchen.

She motions to me to join her in what she is doing. As my

mother did when I was young, she hands me my own ball of dough to roll out with my own rolling pin. She's busy. She doesn't want to talk but to have me do what she does. So I watch her, and together we roll out several large, oblong pieces of dough. She hands me one of my mother's biscuit cutters (where did she get that?), and together we make small rounds of all the dough, placing each circle on a long baking sheet.

When the first batches are in the oven, and we have mixed more dough, she puts the kettle on and motions for me to sit down at the kitchen table. I look around with interest at the house we are in. It is a plain, comfortable house, probably built in the early 1960s, a combination of wood, brick, and worn linoleum, a small window over the kitchen sink, a honeysuckle vine growing across it. There is a stack of books on the oval kitchen table, next to a flowerpot with ivy spilling out of it.

She sets down a cup of tea in front of me and sits down with me. She seems thoughtful as she sips her tea, looking out into the backyard at her garden. I notice that the books on the table are copies of the various documents of Vatican II. I tell her I've been reading *Lumen Gentium* and that it is my favorite Vatican II document. She smiles. I ask her about chapter 8, which was written about her role in the life of the Church. She says that as we grow as God's children, we will see her in clearer and clearer light, as the Holy Spirit leads the Church. She says that in different ages, different emphases are needed for us to grow in our faith and understanding, and therefore, love.

I am thinking about this as the kitchen timer rings. It's time to take more bread out of the oven and put the next batch in. She makes me a sandwich, pats my shoulder, and goes out to clip some roses from her garden. She then arranges these in the box where she is packing the now-cooled little rounds of bread.

She washes her face, straightens her kerchief, and motions for me at the door to come put my sandals on as she is doing. Soon we are walking down the front path with the boxes of the flat little circles we have baked and crossed on the top. We head through the neighborhood and then turn onto a downtown street. We find a small, simple Catholic church. (Did that sign really say "Saint Everyone"?) The Church office is closed for lunch, but the door is open, so we leave our boxes inside.

She wants to pray in the main church, so we head back out and around the corner. A side door is open. She straightens her kerchief, I straighten mine, and we walk into the cool silence, genuflecting. When she stands up to look at me, I notice a slight glow from the tabernacle, and then I glance at her, standing still in the middle of this little church. She is gazing at me, her hands out, the growing glow from the tabernacle illuminating her, until she seems made of that light.

In her dark and lovely eyes, I am suddenly lost in a mighty ocean. I understand the immense capacity of her heart to praise and love God continually. In the thundering roar of waves and the groaning of the deep, I understand her longing for her children to know the joy of Jesus and the conversion of their hearts to love.

I close my eyes, and it seems she takes me through the whole world. Together we move like a gust of wind among people of all ages and races and nations — the suffering, the unfairly treated, the persecuted, the poor, the imprisoned, the used and abused, the addicted, the mentally ill, the troubled, the sick, the ignored, the unloved, those who know not how to love, the violent, the hateful, the selfish and the weak, the frightened, the judgmental, the prideful, and the powerful. Together we touch them all. Sometimes she takes my hand and touches people with my fingers. The cool, sweet wind of the Spirit blows around us and through us, blessing us, blessing those we walk among.

"Jesus is Love, Jesus is Life. Jesus is Peace. Jesus is Truth. Jesus is the Way," she says. "My children, pray, pray, pray." She presses small crosses into each hand. Her heart glows with that same light I saw flowing from the tabernacle at the little church, the light of Jesus, who is the Light of the Church, the Light of the World.

This Divine Breeze, as well as this humble touch and presence of Mary, transforms and unites everyone in Christ, bringing all toward his love, redemption, mercy. This is what she does all day. This is her dream for us.

Now we walk along with the people of God, a holy nation, the Christ-light of the world, as they are praying, working, being sanctified and sanctifying the world in all they do. Then, with flashes of lightning and with peels of thunder, I see Mary standing on the moon, her crown of stars on her head, clothed with the sun. I hear her wailing in the pains of childbirth, and I realize I am crying out with her.

And then we are again standing in this little church, two women of small stature, each a little dusty with flour, in spite of our best efforts. But people are coming in to Mass now. I try to recover myself, and breathe normally. I shake my head to clear it.

"If you went to Mass, where would you sit?" I ask her, looking around, wondering what to do.

"I do come to Mass. And I sit with everyone else. Today I will sit with you."

We sit near the back, and she attends devoutly, listening carefully to the word of God, saying the responses and making all the gestures with us. She receives Holy Communion with quiet devotion, and prays intensely afterward. She sings all the hymns with us. She holds my hand.

I recognized the bread we had made as it was consecrated and changed, by the priest in the Person of Christ, into Jesus' Body and Blood, his Soul and Divinity. I am beginning to understand chapter 8 of *Lumen Gentium* as it has unfolded in our day together. She squeezes my arm.

We greet people as we walk out into the fresh air and sunshine. She takes the hand of the priest, pressing it to her cheek like a mother, and he lets her, humbly. Does he know who she is? I wonder.

She puts her arm around me as we walk home. I reflect on the fact that she is the greatest woman who ever was, or who will ever be — yet she is also a simple servant and friend of God, walking beside me in worn sandals. I fall to my knees at her feet. I take hold of the hem of her long blue skirt, touch it to my face, and kiss it. This time she lets me, though. And she laughs.

Come to Mary's House

What is going on at her house today? What is she doing? What does she want of you? Ask her. Follow her through the house, into the garden, or wherever she wants to go. Help her with tasks. Listen to her, learn from her. Relax and be receptive, allowing this scene to unfold before the eyes of your soul for a while.

Epilogue

The thing about coming to Mary's House is that she will start showing up at your house, too. You might come home to find the furniture rearranged, the carpet pulled up, the walls repainted!

Jesus likes the windows open. So now the Holy Spirit is blowing through . . . scattering all of your papers, all those boring forms, bills, and advertisements.

I told you she was sneaky, didn't I?

I also said you would love it!

And you do, don't you?

Acknowledgments

This little book would never have happened without Joseph White and Mary Beth Giltner of Our Sunday Visitor. May the Lord reward them from his vast treasury of graces as I could never thank or repay them enough.

My gratitude also belongs to the early encouragers of my writing: my parents and stepparents, Tim Manning, Mary Hohl, Delphia Wallace, and Tom Heck; my brother, Mark Manning; my high school creative writing teacher, Linda Coats; my "wonderful mama-in-law," Ann Chapman; and my late husband, Bob Chapman. Thanks to Juan Polomo for mentoring, encouraging, and inspiring me as a writer. I thank my daughters and my nephew Stefan for their support and for listening to and reading my work so often. Thanks to the Catholic boy who taught me the Hail Mary and who became my husband (also late) and the father of my children, Marc Blaze Pauc.

Thanks to Lauren Gulde and Julia Motekaitis for persuading me to write publicly for the first time, and to Jason Elizando and Cristobal Almanza for giving me my first place to do so at the (now defunct) Austin Catholic New Media. My love and thanks to Kelly Brown, former editor of my hometown paper, *The Eagle*, for giving me a column and mentoring me, and to Darren Benson, our present editor for keeping me on and being supportive.

My thanks and undying loyalty and love to The Pontifical Biblical Institute of the Holy Hippie Sisterhood: Amy Minke, Andrea Hendon, Jocelyn Jones, Nan Prikryl (yes, that Nan!), Shawna Marcontel, and Paula Countryman for your love, support, inspiration, and friendship these many years.

Thank you to my OCDS. Carmelite Family, The Community of St. Teresa Benedicta of the Cross in Austin, for my Carmelite formation and their steadfast, joyful love and companionship, and for their support of my soul and my writing always, particularly Olga Mort for sourcing a few of the quotes I used at the last minute.

Thanks to everyone at Casa Vides (with Annunciation

House in El Paso) for the "Border Awareness Experience" that inspired one of the devotional entries in this book, especially Chris Davis, Sister Bea and Sister Caroline, Reuben Garcia, and all of the Sisters and volunteers and the guests at the shelters. It is truly Mary's House. Thanks to my traveling companions of the Catholic Coalition for Migrants and Refugees of the Archdiocese of Milwaukee, especially Sr. Ann Catherine.

Thanks to Argenis and Angel Aguilar for letting me write about their late mother, Gloria Diaz, in this book.

Thanks to my soul brothers, Fr. Gregory Ross, OCDS, and Fr. John McMannamon, SJ, for their suggestions, inspiration, and help with this book. Thanks to Bishop Mike Sis, Bishop David Konderla, Fr. Dean Wilhelm, Dcn. Ron Fernandes and his wife, Rita, and Dcn. Frank Ashly for their spiritual guidance, encouragement, support, and care of my soul all of these years.

To those who read and helped me with my work as beta readers ("Mary's Test Kitchen") Anne Boehm, Molly Goldfein, Ann Latour, Julia Motekaitis, Mark Hudgins, Beth Ann Thibodeaux, Julian McMurrey, Gretchen Sams, Allen Hebert, Angela Florian, Letisha Alba, Esther Miranda, and my brother-in-law, Frank Pauc, my profound thanks for their generosity with their time and their helpful feedback.

With heartfelt gratitude I thank artist and friend Michelle

Pena for her beautiful and unique work on this book.

Thank you from my heart to Laurie Malashanko for her elegant developmental editing and kindly support and help.

And to all of my readers, I thank you.

Appendix
Beginning Mental Prayer

All I need is Jesus, His will, and silence.

— St. Maryam of Jesus Crucified
Maryam: The Little Arab, Amédée Bruno, SCJ

First, go somewhere that is quiet enough so you can concentrate and be alone and uninterrupted for a few minutes. Minimize distractions and extraneous noise. Set a timer (for example, for five, fifteen, or thirty minutes) so you can let go and not worry about anything else. The timer will call you back to your day when it is time.

If you are not used to mental prayer, start with a short amount of time. Every minute is one God can work with, and you are more likely to have satisfaction in prayer and make it part of your life if you feel you can succeed.

Sit in a comfortable, supported position. This will help you not have to worry about your body and to relax while you pray.

Calm your body and mind. Put your hands in your lap. Close your eyes.

Take a deep breath. Hold it. Then slow down your breathing. Pay attention to all the sounds around you — sounds outside, sounds in the room, the sound of your breathing. You might think to yourself as you breathe in, "I let go," and as you breathe out, "and I let God."

Relax anywhere you feel tense. Tune in to God's presence with you in this place now, to his peace in and around you. Do what works for you to relax so you can be receptive to God.

You may wish to pray: *Here I am, Mary. I unite myself to your heart, your prayer, your love, to cherish the Lord within me.*

Choose one of these methods of contemplative prayer or another one, whatever works best for you.

Prayer of Recollection

"This prayer is called 'recollection,' because the soul collects its faculties together and enters within itself to be with its God" (St. Teresa of Ávila, *The Way of Perfection*).

The Prayer of Recollection is a method of prayer that St. Teresa of Ávila said the Lord himself had taught her, and that she never knew what it was to pray with satisfaction until she learned it. A complicated version of this prayer was popularized in the seventeenth century, but in my experience a simpler, freer way is much more user-friendly. It is also closer to Teresa's actual description in chapter 26 of *The Way of Perfection*.

First, make the Sign of the Cross and place yourself in the presence of God within you.

Next, make an examination of conscience and pray the Act of Contrition. If you don't have much time, a heartbeat or two of contrition will do. This is simply putting yourself humbly in reality and letting go of any barrier or mask between you and God so he can see your beautiful face, even if, like a good parent, he has to wipe your nose a little. He doesn't mind. He loves you. Allow him to tend to you. Then, with trust in his mercy, place all of your burdens and sins in his hands so that you may be all his.

"Imagine that he is there with you," says Saint Teresa, "and look at him."

Pray a slow, silent, attentive Our Father with Jesus. Pay attention to the words you are saying, and to whom you are saying them, fixing your inner gaze on the Lord in whatever way works for you. In this way, go over the words of the prayer silently, keeping your awareness with Jesus.

Next, let yourself say whatever you need to say to Jesus. Is there anything you need to tell him? Your troubles, your questions, your gratitude? Would you like to tell him that you love him? Tell him whatever is in your heart.

If it is difficult to keep the eyes of your soul on him, try imagining you are with him during parts of his life. If you are sad, be with Jesus as he carries his cross and keep him company. Saint Teresa points out that, such is his love, he will look at you with "eyes of compassion" even then.

Or imagine you are the Samaritan woman at the well and Jesus is thirsty. Give him something to drink. Ask him for living water.

Eventually, when it feels right, segue into interior silence. Just be quiet with God, staying present to him.

Your mind is going to go everywhere. Don't worry. When your brain starts worrying, remembering, planning, dreaming, gently bring it back each time you notice it straying.

Use some simple means of "looking" again at Jesus every time. Silently say his Name. Imagine him with you. Or just remember his tenderness and love are with you in this moment.

You may wish to repeat a phrase from Scripture, such as "Come, Lord Jesus," to help yourself remain in intentional contact with him.

You may wish to close your time of prayer with a "Glory be."

Lectio Divina

To pray *lectio divina*, you will need:

- A Bible passage
- A notebook and something to write with (optional)
- An open, receptive heart

You might begin, after the Sign of the Cross, with a prayer to the Holy Spirit such as "Come Holy Spirit."

Step 1: *Lectio*

Choose a Scripture passage ahead of time. I usually choose something from the Mass readings of the day.

Read the passage aloud, slowly and reflectively.

As you hear the Scripture passage, listen for a word, phrase, or sentence that stands out to you. (Don't worry, one will.)

After the third time reading the passage through, write your word or phrase in the notebook, or just keep it in mind.

The Benedictine monks who developed this prayer form called this notebook of verses a "florilegium," meaning "book of flowers." Writing your verse or phrase down can help you focus as you pray, and it may be fruitful for later perusal, discussion with soul friends, or for future prayer and reflection.

Step 2: *Meditatio*

This time will be silent, eyes closed.

Inwardly repeat your word or phrase with expectation. As you ponder it, ask God to show you what he is saying to you with this verse. Let yourself be guided by the Holy Spirit, allowing him to make clear his message to you.

With the Holy Spirit's guidance, apply this message to your life and relationship with God.

When your mind wanders, gently bring it back to your word or phrase, placing yourself once more in God's presence.

Step 3: *Oratio*

Respond with a silent prayer back to God about what he has led you to understand or given to you during *meditatio*. Have a conversation with him about it.

You might wish to write your prayer response into your notebook and/or to pray it aloud.

Step 4: *Contemplatio*

Contemplation usually means to rest in God's heart in silence. Close your eyes, place yourself in the presence of God, and rest lovingly there together with him.

If it is hard for you to do this, you might choose a very short prayer, such as the names of Jesus or Mary, perhaps your favorite name for God, or "Christ have mercy," for your mind to hold onto like a walking stick as it travels in quiet over the next few minutes.

When your time is up, you may wish to pray the Our Father. End with the Sign of the Cross.

Meditatio Scripturarum

This is a method of prayer practiced by the Desert Fathers and Mothers. It is simple and based on faith in the power and life of God's word. In this prayer, we take a passage of Scripture we have memorized and hold it in our hearts, turning it over and over. We leave what it does up to God, whose word never returns to him void, but always does what he sends it to do (se Is 55:11). We silently "hear" it, and cherish it intentionally in our hearts as a communion with God, without analysis. We simply allow the Sower to sow the seed, prayerfully tending the soil to encourage deep roots.

Desert Father Abba Poemen said, "The nature of water is soft; that of stone is hard. But if a bottle is hung above the stone, allowing the water to fall drop by drop, it wears away the stone" (*Sayings of the Desert Fathers*). When we continually ponder the word of God, it will surely soften and open our hearts to its mystery.

Choosing a Passage

To begin with, choose a passage you especially love or feel drawn to, or maybe one that seems to speak to your current life situation. Make it the average length of a psalm or canticle — not too short, not too long. If you are in crisis or in discernment about something, you may want to ask someone else to prayerfully choose a passage for you — a spiritual director, a priest, or a friend, trusting in the Holy Spirit to work through that person. You may want to follow the lectionary, and let the Holy Spirit lead you in the daily Mass readings of the liturgical year. We should make sure we don't habitually pick passages that suit our self-will, but remain receptive so we can be good soil.

Memorizing

I like writing a passage out and keeping it in my pocket all day to read and go over again and again. Read it right before going to sleep. Work on it when you're filling the car with gas, standing in line at the grocery store, or at a boring meeting.

Meditating

Once you are recollected, begin to go mentally over the passage very slowly — not too slowly, but don't rush through it, either. You will find your perfect pace and phrasing. He humbled himself taking the form of a slave being born in the likeness of men (see Phil 2:8).

Let the phrases be like a string of rosary beads slipping slowly through your fingers. When you get to the end of your verse, phrase, or passage, begin again.

If you are distracted, just bring yourself gently back to the words. A small distraction merits gentle redirection, picking up where you left off. But if your mind has completely left the passage and is doing its own thing, firmly start again at the beginning. It works, and over time you will have fewer and fewer distractions.

This is time you spend in intimacy with God, attentive to his word, quietly and tenderly resting in him and allowing him to rest also in you.

"Mono-Syllabic" Prayer

Outlined in The Cloud of Unknowing, *a fourteenth-century guide to interior prayer by an anonymous monastic author.*

> For silence is not God, nor speaking; fasting is not God, nor eating; solitude is not God, nor company; nor any other pair of opposites. God is hidden between them and cannot be found by anything your soul does, but

only by the love of your heart. God cannot be known by reason, nor by thought, caught, or sought by understanding. But God can be loved and chosen by the true, loving will of your heart. (anonymous author, *The Cloud of Unknowing*)

The author teaches that, in our current state of fallenness, God dwells for us in a "cloud of unknowing." In this prayer, we create for ourselves a "cloud of forgetting," setting within it our thoughts, imagination, worries, even all that God made in favor of pure encounter with God himself, not anything he has made, not anything we may want, just for now.

The following method of prayer is drawn from chapters 3–7 of *The Cloud*:

To begin, lift up your heart to God with "a humble stirring of love." Don't think thoughts about God, rather use one syllable — "God" or "Love" — to reach out to him in simplicity. If there is a one syllable word that means more to you, the author says you may use that, only it should be only one syllable. This will be your "dart" or "spark" of love flying straight to the Heart of God. Sit quietly, attentive to him. Whenever your attention wanders, or distractions assail you, use your syllable — "God" or "Love" or another one you have chosen — to bring yourself back to your loving attentiveness to him.

Tune in for a time to the silent love that flows between you. Only love him, and let yourself be loved. This is all you need to do.

A Final Word of Encouragement

Whoever has not begun the practice of prayer, I beg for the love of the Lord not to go without so great a good. There is nothing here to fear but only something to desire.

— St. Teresa of Ávila, *The Book of Her Life*

In the first place it should be known that if a person is seeking God, his beloved is seeking him much more.

— St. John of the Cross, *Living Flame of Love*

What does it feel like to practice mental prayer? It can seem a little strange when you first begin because you are not used to it. It may be peaceful but hard to keep up as a habit. You may feel anxious or self-conscious. You may feel as if you are drowning in distractions. You may think "I can't do this. I'm not one of those people who can do this kind of thing."

Despite any negative thoughts or feelings, I urge you to have faith and plug on. Some people have intense consolations in prayer. Don't worry if you do, don't worry if you don't. The most important thing is not to let either ordinariness or consolations in prayer stop or distract you from your purpose of simple faith, hope, and love, of your gift of self to God. God knows just what you need, and he will provide it.

Don't worry about how well you think you are praying or if you think your prayer time is going badly. God's power is never limited by our perception of how our prayer is going.

For a long time, as Saint Teresa points out, we will have to draw and haul water for the garden of our souls. In time, we find ways to irrigate this garden with much less work, and we have more divine assistance. By the grace of God and him willing it, eventually, it simply rains as the soul is graced with passive prayer that comes from God. "I am the Lord your God who brought you out of Egypt. Open your mouth wide, and I will fill it" (Ps 81:10).

The Father, the Son, and the Holy Spirit, Mary, and all of the saints are here with you to help you on this journey. You are not alone. Don't hesitate to ask for their help.

There are obstacles and potholes along the royal road of

prayer. Let nothing stop you. Rather, like Mary, be continually amazed. Follow the ways of prayer with her sense of wonder and gratitude, and you will overcome.

We can spend a lot of time being mad at ourselves and feeling unworthy of this path. We all go through those stages. Try having a sense of patient affection with yourself, as you would with a child you love. This approach will help you create a little detachment from yourself that is more productive in the spiritual life than being bogged down with self-recrimination. That kind of thinking will only lead you away from being with God. Practice letting it go into his hands and praying anyway.

Busyness is a real problem for those of us who want to build a life of prayer. Our Lord understands. He knows. The important thing is to do the best you can, and not give up! For a while you may be disciplined and consistent. Then something might happen that throws you out of whack for a bit. During my years as a single mom of little children, I grabbed the time I could — even five or ten minutes here and there, but God worked with me. He can work with you, too. Do what you can, and look for paths forward, trusting his will.

In the end, prayer is really about love. God sees the love you have in your commitment, whatever the method or lack of method, whatever you are able to do or give. As Saint Teresa says in *The Way of Perfection*, "Just look at Him!"

If you run into a dry patch (this is called "aridity") and prayer feels like reading the phone book, just remember that Jesus is in the Temple doing the Father's work, whatever you feel. You can trust that. You will grow tremendously by continuing in patience and faith, no matter what.

So many of us are living with broken hearts these days. I can witness to the fact that there is nothing more healing than to present our hearts as they are to God and begin letting him in. In a patient, trusting way, sit still and let him love you, letting yourself love him.

The seeds of healing God plants in us scatter as from a dandelion blown by the Holy Spirit, to be planted in hearts all over the world.

Remember, Mary arose and went with haste to visit Elizabeth! So don't wait to begin mental prayer! Don't wait until your schedule clears, until you figure this prayer stuff out, or you have a prayer corner set up, more confidence, a regular holy hour, or a perfect life. Don't wait until you go to confession. Don't wait until tomorrow! Arise and go with haste to meet the Lord in inner prayer. Take Mary's hand now, and don't wait any longer to join her in prayer from the heart.

Come to Mary's House. Learn from her how to make Jesus

smile. Say to her:

O beautiful flower of Carmel,
Most Fruitful vine,
Holy and singular,
Who did bring forth the Son of God,
Ever still remaining a pure virgin,
Assist us in our necessity,
O Star of the Sea,
Help and protect us.
Show us that thou art our mother!
Our Lady of Mount Carmel,
Pray for us.

About the Author

Shawn Chapman is the mother of two young adult daughters, enthusiastic grandmother of three small children, and a Discalced Carmelite Secular. She is the Catholic columnist for the *Bryan-College Station Eagle* newspaper and a caregiver. She likes hanging out with friends, reading, writing, listening to music, taking long walks, and cooking awesome vegan food. She is a native Texan where she lives with her younger daughter and her child, as well as two cats and several plants, and near her elder daughter and her two children.

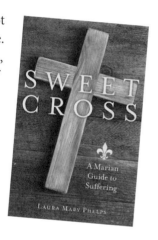

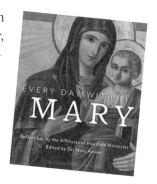